Harold Boulton

Songs of the four nations

A collection of old songs of the people of England, Scotland, Ireland and Wales

Harold Boulton

Songs of the four nations

A collection of old songs of the people of England, Scotland, Ireland and Wales

ISBN/EAN: 9783337266158

Printed in Europe, USA, Canada, Australia, Japan

Cover: Foto ©Thomas Meinert / pixelio.de

More available books at **www.hansebooks.com**

SONGS OF THE FOUR NATIONS.

A Collection of Old Songs of the
People of England, Scotland, Ireland and Wales,
For the most part never before published with complete
Words and Accompaniments.

Edited by

HAROLD BOULTON,

With Traditional Words or Original Poems and Translations by
Nicholas Bennett, Harold Boulton,
Rev. Owen Davies (Eos Llechyd), F. A. Fahy,
A. P. Graves, Dr. Douglas Hyde and
G. M. Probert.

The Music Arranged by

ARTHUR SOMERVELL.

J. B. CRAMER & Co.,
201, Regent Street,
London.
mdcccxcii.

*Dedicated
by
Gracious Permission
to
HER MAJESTY
The Queen.*

SONGS OF THE FOUR NATIONS.

PREFACE.

THIS volume is the result of a pilgrimage taken in congenial company through the region of veritable fairyland that forms the musical heritage of our native islands. In "Songs of the North," in which the present editor also bore a part, were gathered together the fruits of an expedition similarly entered upon in which one portion only of the kingdom was concerned. The quantity of beautiful melodies, hitherto little known, which were then brought to light, made it appear probable that if the range of research were enlarged, England, Scotland, Ireland and Wales might still yield much musical treasure well worth preserving and presenting to a modern audience in available form. Nor has the expectation been disappointed.

The fifty songs here set down have been selected from among thousands of others, and the desire has been that they may appear in a manner acceptable to our own ears and voices, without losing the spontaneity and freshness which made them dear to our forefathers. To obtain this result an honest effort has been made throughout.

In grouping the "Songs of the Four Nations," in accordance with their origin, it soon became apparent that the division into England, Scotland, Wales, and Ireland, was not sufficiently accurate. There was not only the obvious distinction to be drawn between the Highlands and Lowlands of Scotland, but also the difference between Cornwall and the rest of England, in the fact that up to recent times the Duchy had preserved among other distinctive characteristics her separate branch of the Celtic language. In addition to this there was the separate existence as a people claimed by the inhabitants of the Isle of Man, sufficiently justified by their own national institutions and government, and the Celtic speech that still lingers among them.

It is felt to be a subject of congratulation by the collectors of these melodies, that they have been able to include here songs (with English equivalents in every instance) in all the five Celtic tongues belonging respectively to Cornwall, the Highlands of Scotland, Wales, Ireland, and the Isle of Man.

Though it is claimed that the contents of this book fully represent the individuality and beauty of the national music hailing from all parts of our country, they are not, as a rule, identical with those found in current collections. A large proportion have dropped out of common cognisance even where they were once well-known.

It will be observed however that some half-dozen songs out of the fifty are old established favourites, and the excuse, if any be needed, for their presence, is the irresistible impulse which has been felt in certain cases to handle once more in what is deemed the best fashion some well-loved master-theme; but in dealing with themes whether familiar or unfamiliar, both editor and musician have striven to be true to the particular spirit and genius contained therein. Where words have been lost, or obviously incongruous words of more modern date than the tune have taken the place of the original song, an attempt has been made to work upon older models; the same rule has been applied to old words which have been divorced from their original tunes, and wedded to more modern ones.

As an instance of the perverse disregard for accuracy which has sometimes distinguished adapters of national melodies, may be mentioned the fact that one air, "The Happy Farmer," among the most essentially English in this collection, was unearthed in an old edition of so-called "Scottish Songs." Any consideration that might have remained for the opinion of the aforesaid adapter was dispelled by the present editor being fortunate enough to come across a recent criticism on the work in question by the Rev. S. Baring-Gould, a careful authority on such matters, who remarks that "Within the first twenty-four songs of the first volume are compositions by Purcell, Arne, Hook, Berg, and Battishill."

In the present case no partiality has been felt or needed for anything except strict historical accuracy as far as it is possible in describing the old melodies dealt with. Those interested in the subject will observe that the old English words of "My Lodging it is on the Cold Ground," do not appear in conjunction with the tune, claimed as Irish, with which they have latterly been associated, but with the old English tune to which, as far as we know, they originally belonged.

The words of each song have been printed at length on a separate page as well as under the musical notation, in order that where only a few verses of a song are necessary for singing the poem may also appear as a whole. In the case of the Celtic nationalities, the Celtic appears side by side with the English version.

Much fascination might be found in studying the evidences of various race characteristics, the circumstances of time and place, and other incidental conditions underlying the genius of national music. Some will remark the breezy joviality and complacency of many old English songs, though the English muse has her moments of regretful melancholy too, which unite her possibly with the weird imagination of Scandinavian ancestry; others will be struck with the delicate sweetness of Lowland Scottish minstrelsy, the wild and rugged beauty of Highland song, the sophisticated melodial rhythm of Welsh music, or the curious alternations of wild pathos and homely wit discoverable in passing from one Irish song to another. Speaking in a more strictly musical sense, the curious will discern turns of melody and methods of construction markedly peculiar to one country or the other; take for example the constant successive iteration of the key-note at the close of so many Irish melodies; in countless songs the tonic is repeated two or three, and in some instances four, or even five times, as a conclusion to the melody.

It is to be feared that many who aspire to fame as composers are woefully ignorant of the nature of that glorious wealth of native music and musical tradition which their patriotism ought to suggest as a groundwork for their musical development however skilled and elaborate. The names will at once suggest themselves of various foreign masters who have conspicuously shown in their work an individuality in conformity with their own origin; it seems almost a truism to insist that the genius of any great national composer among ourselves must spring from and be nurtured upon native and not foreign impulses.

The patriotic assistance given to the preparation of this volume by those best qualified to do so in every part of the kingdom cannot be too gratefully acknowledged. The names which follow are an integral part of this preface, because they record the essential labour of those who have helped to build up the book.

In English Song valuable sympathy and help has been given by Mr. Fuller Maitland, Miss Wakefield, Mr. W. H. Hadow, of Oxford, and the Rev. S. Baring-Gould, whose special knowledge of Devonian and Cornish folk-lore has been of assistance, among other things, in procuring the West of England melody with Cornish words which represents in this collection that portion of the country.

For help in *Highland Song* thanks are due to the Mackintosh of Mackintosh; Miss Campbell of Glendaruel, and Mr. D. Mackintosh, Inverness, who, in conjunction with the Gaelic Society of the Highland capital, has been at pains to furnish correct versions of Gaelic songs.

In *Scottish Song* Miss Wakefield has helped greatly; also Miss Liza Lehmann (who took down orally a beautiful melody); Miss Hamilton of Sundrum; Mr. Charles White, Alva; Mr. Bruce J. Home, late of Edinburgh; and Messrs. Patterson & Co., of that city.

For the *Welsh* portion of the volume thanks are primarily due to the enthusiastic work of Mr. W. M. Roberts, Wrexham, whose musical and literary attainments (the latter in two languages) are well known both within and beyond the principality; Mr. Nicholas Bennett, of Glanyrafon, a long established authority on Welsh song, and himself a poet, has added to the store a Welsh poem from his own pen; the Rev. Owen Davies (Eos Llechyd), an authority of equal eminence, has done a similar service. Thanks are also accorded to Col. Cornwallis West, Lord Lieutenant of Denbighshire, and to Mr. Thomas Roberts, Llangalaford, Ruthin.

Among *Irishmen* Dr. Norman Moore gave much valuable assistance from his wealth of Irish scholarship and devotion to his national literature. The work of two Irish poets, Mr. A. P. Graves and Mr. F. A. Fahy, speaks for itself; Dr. Douglas Hyde is also to be heartily thanked for his poems in the ancient Irish tongue. Kind help has also been given by Sir Robert Stewart, Mus. Doc., Professor of Music at the University of Dublin; and Mr. Michael Scott, Dromore, Co. Kerry.

Last but not least in the list comes that most enthusiastic of *Manxmen*, Mr. Hall Caine, who was kind enough to put within reach a fine melody belonging to the Isle of Man.

The time and thought spent upon the collaboration of this song-book has been in no small measure repaid by the charm of personal intercourse on their native soil with so many well-wishers. The consequent acquisition of local colouring has made the editorship of "Songs of the Four Nations" a delightful task.

Finally all concerned in the gathering of this national garland will feel loyal gratification from the fact that the Sovereign of the Realm has been graciously pleased to accept it as dedicated to herself.

HAROLD BOULTON.

ON THE SINGING OF NATIONAL SONGS.

T is solely with regard to the qualities of singing and expression, common to all forms of music, not to the technique of singing, that I, who am no singer, venture to offer a few remarks.

The first thing to be remembered is the extreme simplicity of the national tune. It takes in music the same place as the simplest lyric takes in poetry. It is as absurd to try to sing it with great dramatic intensity, as it would be to try to read "It was a lover and his lass," in the manner of a scene from Hamlet. In a reading of the poem, the whole virtue consists in keeping intact the bird-song idea of this lyric; the transitoriness of love and springtime is so lightly touched by the poet as to be quite subordinate to the warbling sound of the song. It answers absolutely to Mr. F. T. Palgrave's definition of a lyric, that it "shall turn on some single thought, feeling, or situation." So with National Songs; the tunes are of the simplest possible construction, and are repeated again and again, quite regardless of the varying character of the words. And herein lies the difficulty of singing them; the monotony being often made the excuse for violating every rule of time, rhythm, common sense, and good taste. Such songs as these, have, for the larger part, sprung anonymously from the people, and, handed down by them, have sufficed to express their narrow (not necessarily shallow), range of feeling on the subjects of love, war, and other primary emotions of mankind. Is it not therefore manifestly absurd to try to lash into, and wrench out of them, the kind of passion and sentiment appropriate to a great song which is the finished product of such supreme latter-day artists as Schumann or Brahms?

It is surely a cheap and easy way out of the difficulty of singing a simple song, to try and make it *not* simple, and so lose its first characteristic.

The following is a National Air as I have heard it sung by a great singer. In the programme, it was entered as "The Last Rose of Summer."

This is the kind of thing which is called "getting vocal effects." It is an absurd thing to do, and should be as emphatically damned by a musical audience, as a violinist would be, who paused for three or four bars on a crotchet in the middle of a piece because he happened to get a better tone than usual on that note.

To those amateurs who wish to sing National Songs with musical intelligence, and to give pleasure to those who listen, and who cannot go to a really musicianly teacher of singing to learn each song, I should recommend that they should (1) carefully look at the tune and words, and determine what is the leading idea running through the song. Is it, as in "Scots wha hae," a battle march, or as in "Mary Jamieson," a love lament; or as in "The Tree in the Wood," a mystic, dreamy legend? Let this leading characteristic dominate the whole rendering of the song. (2) Get the rhythm well into your head, and play over the song to yourself in such strict time and rhythm, that a village audience could stamp its feet to the tune; and afterwards, never forget this rhythm, even during a *rallentando*. (3) Then study carefully what scope is given in the tune and the accompaniment, to express the changes of sentiment of the words. And finally always think of the song as a whole, and do not exhaust your effects before the final climax, should there be one. Then within the limits of time and rhythm, put into your singing all the expression or feeling you can give.

Remember that the scope for feeling is limited, and that therefore the expression of it is best given by a few delicate, forcible touches.

It is hard to say exactly in what expression consists. It is easier to say that it is *not* in absence of rhythm, it is *not* in entire absence of time, it is *not* in violent emphasis of unimportant notes or words; in a word, it is not in the vulgarity of extremes.

ARTHUR SOMERVELL.

Songs of the Four Nations.

CONTENTS.

English.

		Authors.	Airs.	Page.
I.	Ye Mariners of England	Thomas Campbell	By Dr. Calcott	2
II.	Thou wilt not go and leave me here	Unknown	Thou wilt not go and leave me here	8
III.	When the King Enjoys His Own Again	Harold Boulton	When the King enjoys his own again	14
IV.	Cupid's Garden	Unknown	Cupid's Garden	20
V.	My Lodging it is on the Cold Ground	Unknown	My Lodging it is on the cold ground	24
VI.	Old Towler	Unknown	Old Towler	30
VII.	Floodes of Tears	Unknown	Floodes of Tears	36
VIII.	Pretty Polly Oliver	Harold Boulton	Pretty Polly Oliver	40
IX.	Three Ravens (The)	Unknown	The Three Ravens	46
X.	Happy Farmer (The)	Harold Boulton	The Happy Clown	52

Cornish.

XI.	Where be Going?	Unknown	Where be going?	58

Scottish.

XII.	Doun in yon Bank	Harold Boulton	Doune in yon banke	62
XIII.	Here's to Thy Health	Robert Burns	Laggan Burn	66
XIV.	Oh! She's Bonnie!	Unknown	Gently blaw ye Eastern breezes	70
XV.	Blink over the Burn	Robert Allan	Blink over the Burn	74
XVI.	Scots wha hae	Robert Burns	Hey Tuttie Taitie	78
XVII.	Mary Jamieson	Unknown	Mary Jamieson	81
XVIII.	Twine the Plaiden	Unknown	Twine the Plaiden	88
XIX.	Will ye no come back again?	Lady Nairne	Will ye no come back again?	94
XX.	In Yon Garden	Unknown	In yon garden	100
XXI.	Were na My Heart Licht	Lady Grizell Baillie	Were na my heart licht	104

Highland.

XXII.	Isle of the Heather (The)	Gaelic—*M. Macleod* / English translation—*Harold Boulton*	The Isle of the Heather	110
XXIII.	The Mackintosh's Lament	Gaelic—Unknown / English translation—*Harold Boulton*	The Mackintosh's Lament	115

Welsh.

XXIV.	Opening of the Key (The)	English—*Harold Boulton* / Welsh simile—*G. M. Probert*	The Opening of the Key	122
XXV.	Slender Boy (The)	English—*Harold Boulton* / Welsh simile—*G. M. Probert*	The Slender Boy	128
XXVI.	All Through the Night	English—*Harold Boulton* / Welsh simile—*G. M. Probert*	All through the Night	134
XXVII.	Dimpled Cheek (The)	English—Unknown / Welsh simile—*G. M. Probert*	The Dimpled Cheek	

CONTENTS.—*Continued.*

Welsh.—*Continued.*

		Authors.	Airs.	Page.
XXVIII.	By the Waters of Babylon ...	English, Psalm, cxxxvii, adapted by Arthur Somervell ... ... Welsh paraphrase—*G. M. Probert* ...	By the Waters of Babylon ...	... 144
XXIX.	Gwenllian ...	Welsh—*Nicholas Bennett* ... English translation—*Harold Boulton*	Gwenllian ...	... 150
XXX.	Jenny's Mantle ...	English—*Harold Boulton* ... Welsh simile—*G. M. Probert*	Jenny's Mantle ...	... 154
XXXI.	Gwilym and Ellen ...	English—Unknown ... Welsh simile—*G. M. Probert*	Gwilym and Ellen ...	... 160
XXXII.	Mistletoe (The) ...	English—*Harold Boulton* ... Welsh simile—*G. M. Probert*	The Woodbunch ...	... 164
XXXIII.	Melody of May (The)	English—*Harold Boulton* ... Welsh simile—*G. M. Probert*	The Melody of May...	... 168
XXXIV.	Dream of Little Rhys ...	Welsh—*Rev. Owen Davies* (Eos Llechyd) English translation—*Harold Boulton*	The Dream of Little Rhys ...	... 176
XXXV.	Ash Grove (The) ...	English—*Harold Boulton* ... Welsh simile—*G. M Probert*	The Ash Grove ...	... 180

Manx.

XXXVI.	Myle Charaine ...	Manx—Unknown ... English adaptation—*Harold Boulton*	Myle Charaine ...	... 188

Irish.

		Authors.	Airs.	Page.
XXXVII.	When in Death ...	English—*Thomas Moore* ... Irish translation—*Archbishop MacHale*	The Bard's Legacy ...	... 194
XXXVIII.	Gentle Maiden (The) ...	English—*Harold Boulton* ... Irish translation—*Dr. Douglas Hyde*	The Gentle Maiden...	... 200
XXXIX.	Kitty Magee ...	English—*F. A. Fahy* ...	Kitty Magee ...	... 204
XL.	Shule Agra ...	English—*A. P. Graves* ... Irish translation—*Dr. Douglas Hyde*	Shule Agra ...	... 210
XLI.	Castle of Dromore (The)	English—*Harold Boulton* ... Irish translation—*Dr. Douglas Hyde*	My Wife is Sick ...	... 216
XLII.	Snowy-breasted Pearl (The) ...	Irish—Unknown ... English—*Dr. Petrie* ...	The Snowy-breasted Pearl ...	... 222
XLIII.	Wild Hills of Clare (The)	English—*F. A. Fahy* ... Irish translation—*Dr. Douglas Hyde*	Lament of William McPeter ...	... 226
XLIV.	Little Mary Cassidy ...	English—*F. A. Fahy* ...	The little Stack of Barley ...	... 232
XLV.	Gaol of Clonmel (The) ...	English—*F. A. Fahy* ... Irish translation—*Dr. Douglas Hyde*	Gaol of Clonmel ...	... 238
XLVI.	Drimin Dhu	English—*F. A. Fahy* ... Irish translation—*Dr. Douglas Hyde*	Drimin Dhu ...	... 244
XLVII.	Barney Brallaghan ...	English—*A. P. Graves* ...	Barney Brallaghan ...	... 250
XLVIII.	Tree in the Wood (The)	English—*Harold Boulton* ... Irish translation—*Dr. Douglas Hyde*	The Tree in the Wood ...	... 254
XLIX.	Kathleen ni Hoolhaun ...	Irish—*William Heffernan* ... English adaptation—*F. A. Fahy* ...	Kathleen ni Hoolhaun ...	... 262
L.	Yellow Boreen (The) ...	Irish—Unknown ... English translation—*Dr. Petrie* ...	The Yellow Boreen ...	... 268

N.B.—An Alphabetical Index will be found at the end of the Volume.

ERRATA.

PAGE 5 —Line 2, Bar 1, Right Hand—

PAGE 24.—Line 1, Bar 4, Left Hand, last 2 quavers—

PAGE 37.—Line 4, Bar 3, Voice Part, E, not F.

PAGE 55.—Line 3, Bar 2, Right Hand, last chord—

PAGE 74.—Line 1, Bar 3, Left Hand—

PAGE 83.—Line 2, Bar 3, Right Hand, first two notes—

PAGE 126.—In note at bottom of page, line 2, for *semiquaver* read *quaver*

PAGE 134.—Line 1, Bar 1, Right Hand—

PAGE 188.—Line 3, Bar 4, Right Hand, for A♯ play A♭.

PAGE 204.—Line 1, Bar 3, Right Hand, last quaver—

PAGE 210.—Line 2, Bar 2, Left Hand—

PAGE 211.—Line 2, Bar 1, Voice Part, 1st Note, sing C for A.

PAGE 223, Line 3, Bar 2, Left Hand—

Ye Mariners of England.

(THOMAS CAMPBELL.)

I.

YE MARINERS OF ENGLAND.

N°. 1.

Words by THOMAS CAMPBELL.

Air written by D^R. CALLCOTT.
Arranged by ARTHUR SOMERVELL.

1 Ye mariners of England, That guard our native seas, Whose flag hath braved a thousand years The battle and the breeze!

2 The spirits of your fathers Shall start from every wave! For the deck it was their field of fame, And ocean was their grave.

3 Britannia needs no bulwarks, No towers along the steep, Her march is o'er the mountain waves, Her home is on the deep.

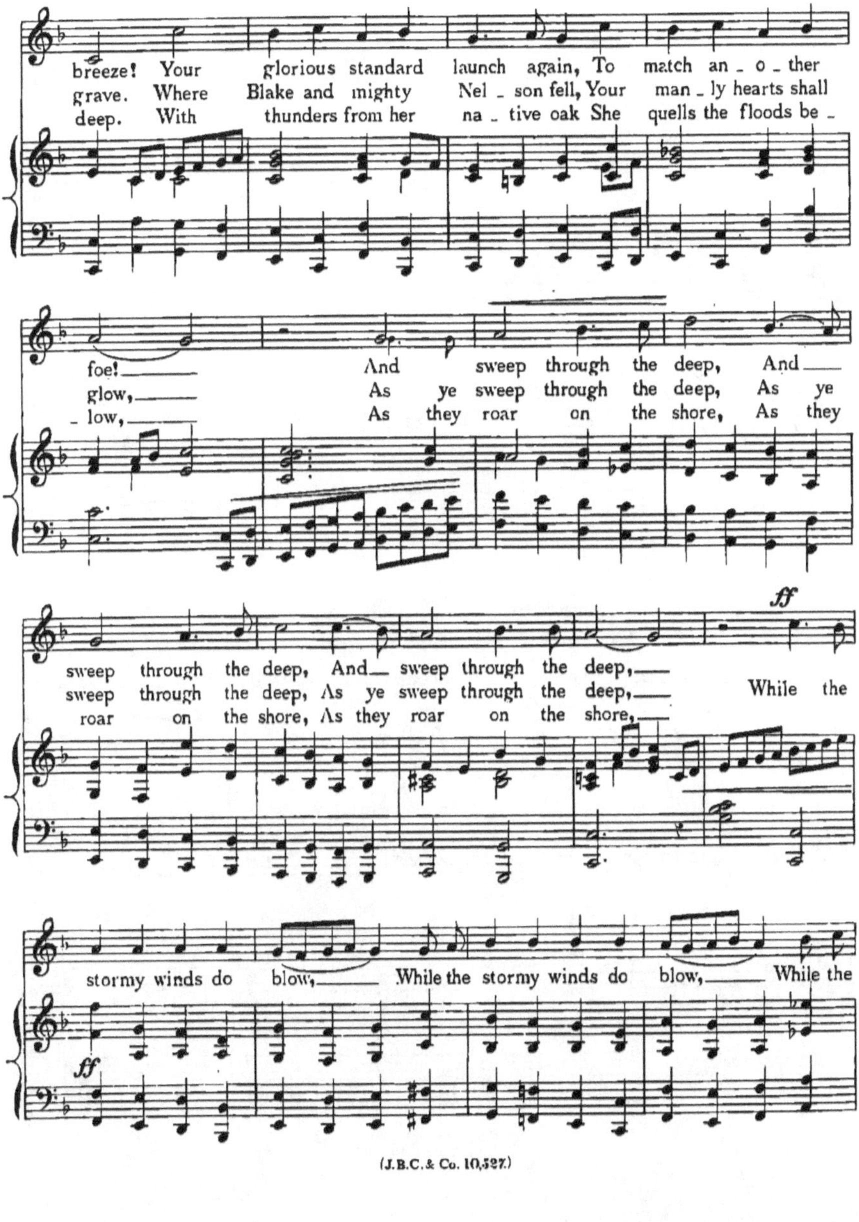
breeze! Your glorious standard launch again, To match an - o - ther
grave. Where Blake and mighty Nel - son fell, Your man - ly hearts shall
deep. With thunders from her na - tive oak She quells the floods be -
foe! And sweep through the deep, And
glow, As ye sweep through the deep, As ye
- low, As they roar on the shore, As they
sweep through the deep, And sweep through the deep,
sweep through the deep, As ye sweep through the deep, While the
roar on the shore, As they roar on the shore,
ff
stormy winds do blow, While the stormy winds do blow, While the
ff

YE MARINERS OF ENGLAND.

Ye Mariners of England!
That guard our native seas,
Whose flag hath braved a thousand years
The battle and the breeze!
Your glorious standard launch again,
To match another foe!
And sweep through the deep,
While the stormy winds do blow;
While the battle rages loud and long,
And the stormy winds do blow.

The spirits of your fathers
Shall start from every wave!
For the deck it was their field of fame,
And ocean was their grave.
Where Blake and mighty Nelson fell,
Your manly hearts shall glow,
As ye sweep through the deep,
While the stormy winds do blow;
While the battle rages loud and long,
And the stormy winds do blow.

Britannia needs no bulwarks,
No towers along the steep;
Her march is o'er the mountain waves,
Her home is on the deep.
With thunders from her native oak,
She quells the floods below,—
As they roar on the shore,
When the stormy winds do blow;
When the battle rages loud and long,
And the stormy winds do blow.

The meteor flag of England
Shall yet terrific burn,
Till danger's troubled night depart,
And the star of peace return.
Then, then, ye ocean-warriors,
Our song and feast shall flow
To the fame of your name,
When the storm has ceased to blow;
When the fiery fight is heard no more,
And the storm has ceased to blow.

THOMAS CAMPBELL.

Thou wilt not go and Leave Me Here.

II.

THOU WILT NOT GO AND LEAVE ME HERE.

Thow wilt not goe and leave me heir,
Oh do not so my dearest deir.
The sune's depairting clouds the sky,
Bot thy depairting maks me die.

Thow can'st not goe, my deirest heart,
Bot I must quyt my choisest pairt;
For with two hearts thou must be gone,
And I sall stay at home with none.

Meanwhill, my pairt sall be to murne,
Telling the houres whill thow returne;
My eyes sall be but eyes to weip,
But nether eyes to sie nor sleipe.

Prevent the hazard of this ill,
Goe not at all, stay with me still;
I'lle bath thy lips with kisses then,
And look for mor ease back againe.

Since thou will needs goe, weill away!
Leave, leave one hart with me to stay;
Take mine, lett thine in pane remaine,
That quicklie thow may come againe.

Fairweill, deir hearte, since it must be,
That thow wilt not remain with me;
My greatest greife it still sall be,
I love a love that loves not me.

TRADITIONAL.
(Spelling as in copy at Advocates
Library, Edinburgh, 1639.)

When the King Enjoys His Own Again.

(HAROLD BOULTON.)

III.

14

No. 3.

WHEN THE KING ENJOYS HIS OWN AGAIN.

Words by
HAROLD BOULTON.

Old English Air arranged by
ARTHUR SOMERVELL.

The worst of wea_ther can_ but_ mend, There's a
Our maidens, come_ly to_ be_ seen, Once

turn_ing to the long_est lane; E'en ras_cal Roundhead
more shall wreathe the May_pole green; Our hon_est fel_lows

(J.B.C. & Co. 10,627.)

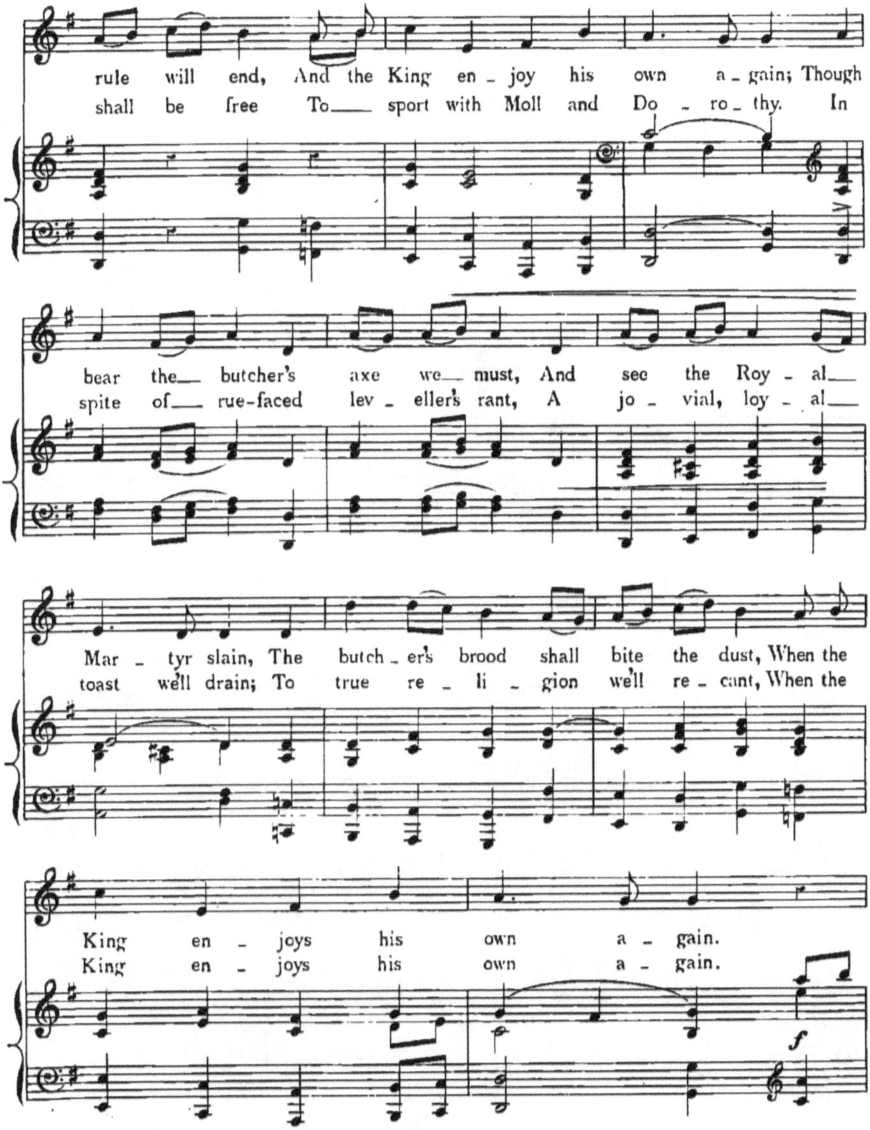
rule will end, And the King en - joy his own a - gain; Though
shall be free To___ sport with Moll and Do - ro - thy. In
bear the___ butcher's axe we___ must, And see the Roy - al___
spite of___ rue-faced lev - eller's rant, A jo - vial, loy - al___
Mar - tyr slain, The butch - er's brood shall bite the dust, When the
toast we'll drain; To true re - li - gion we'll re - cant, When the
King en - joys his own a - gain.
King en - joys his own a - gain.
f

WHEN THE KING ENJOYS HIS OWN AGAIN.

The worst of weather can but mend,
    There's a turning to the longest lane;
E'en rascal Roundhead rule will end,
    And the King enjoy his own again.
Though bear the butcher's axe we must,
    And see the royal martyr slain,
The butcher's brood shall bite the dust,
    When the King enjoys his own again.

Our maidens, comely to be seen,
    Once more shall wreathe the Maypole green;
Our honest fellows shall be free
    To sport with Moll and Dorothy.
In spite of rue-faced levellers' rant,
    A jovial loyal toast we'll drain;
To true religion we'll recant.
    When the King enjoys his own again.

Since England well hath understood
    The Commonwealth is common woe,
Our royal rose once red with blood,
    In rare white majesty shall grow;
Its thorns shall prick the impious hand
    That dared its beauty to disdain,
While peace and plenty bless the land,
    When the King enjoys his own again.

                      HAROLD BOULTON.

Cupid's Garden.

IV.

CUPID'S GARDEN.

'Twas down in Cupid's garden for pleasure I did go,
To see the pretty flowers that in that garden grow;
The first it was the Jessamine, the Lily, Pink, and Rose,
They are the finest flowers that in that garden grows.

I'd not been in Cupid's garden no more than half-an-hour,
When I seed two fine young maidens a sitting in Cupid's bower,
A pulling of the Jessamine, the Lily, Pink, and Rose,
They are the finest flowers that in that garden grows.

I fondly steps to one of them, and thus to her I says,
" Be you engaged to e'er a young man, come tell to me I prays."
" I bean't engaged to ne'er a young man, I solemnly declare,
I aims to be a maiden, and still the laurel wear."

Says I " My stars and garters, why here's a pretty go,
For a fine young maid as ever was to sarve all mankind so."
Then tother young maid looked sly at me, and from her seat she's risen,
Says she " Let us go our own way, and we'll let she go shis'n."

TRADITIONAL.

(This edition of the words was found in Gloucestershire, by Mr. W. H. Hadow,
Dean of Worcester College, Oxford. There are various editions in
Devonshire and elsewhere.)

My Lodging it is on the Cold Ground.

v.

MY LODGING IT IS ON THE COLD GROUND.

My lodging it is on the cold ground,
And hard, very hard is my fare,
But that which troubles me most
Is the coldness of my dear.
Yet still I cry, "Oh turn, love,
And prithee love turn to me,
For thou art the one that I long for,
And alack, what remedy?"

I'll crown thee with garland of straw, love,
I'll marry thee with a rush ring;
My frozen hopes they will thaw then,
And merrily will we sing.
    Yet still I cry, &c., &c.

But if thou wilt harden thy heart still,
All deaf to my pitiful moan,
Then I must endure the smart, dear,
And tumble in straw alone.
    Then still I cry, &c., &c.

TRADITIONAL.

Old Towler.

VI.

33

"OLD TOWLER."

Bright chanticleer proclaims the dawn,
   And spangles deck the thorn;
The lowing herds now quit the lawn,
   The lark springs from the corn.
Dogs, huntsmen, round the window throng,
   Fleet Towler leads the cry;
Arise the burthen of their song,
   "This day a stag must die."

Chorus.   With a hey ho chivey,
        Hark forward, hark forward, tantivy!
        With a hey ho chivey,
        Hark forward, hark forward, tantivy!
        Hark forward, hark forward, hark forward!
        Arise the burthen of their song,
        "This day a stag must die."

The cordial takes its merry round,
   The laugh and joke prevail;
The huntsman blows a jovial sound,
   The dogs sniff up the gale.
The upland winds they sweep along,
   O'er fields, thro' brakes they fly,
The game is roused, too true the song,
   "This day a stag must die."

Chorus.   With a hey ho chivey, etc., etc.

Poor stag, the dogs thy haunches gore,
   The tears run down thy face;
The huntsman's pleasure is no more,
   His joys were in the chase.
Alike the sportsmen of the town,
   A virgin game in view,
Are full content to run them down,
   Then they in turn pursue.

Chorus.   With a hey ho chivey, etc., etc.

TRADITIONAL.

Floodes of Tears.

VII.

FLOODES OF TEARS.

No. 7.

Words Traditional.
Spelling as in Forbes Cantus.

Old English Air arranged by
Arthur Somervell.

If floodes of tears could change my follies past, Or smoaks of sighs could sacrifice for sin,

Since man is nothing but a mass of clay, Our days not else but shadows on the wall,

(J. B. C. & Co. 10527.)

FLOODES OF TEARS.

If floodes of tears could change my follies past,
   Or smoaks of sighs could sacrifice for sin,
If groaning cries could free my fault at last,
   Or endless moan could even pardon win,
Then would I weep, sigh, cry, and even groan,
For follies, faults, for sins and errors done.

I see my hopes are blasted in the bud,
   And find men's favours are like fading flowers;
I find too late that words can do no good,
   But loss of time and languishing of hours.
Thus since I see, I sigh and say therefore,
Hopes, favours, words, begone, beguile no more.

Since man is nothing but a mass of clay,
   Our days not else but shadows on the wall,
Trust in the Lord, who lives and reigns for aye,
   Whose favour found will neither fade nor fall.
My God, to Thee, I resign my mouth and mind,
No trust in youth, nor faith in age I find.

                                TRADITIONAL.

Pretty Polly Oliver.

(HAROLD BOULTON.)

VIII.

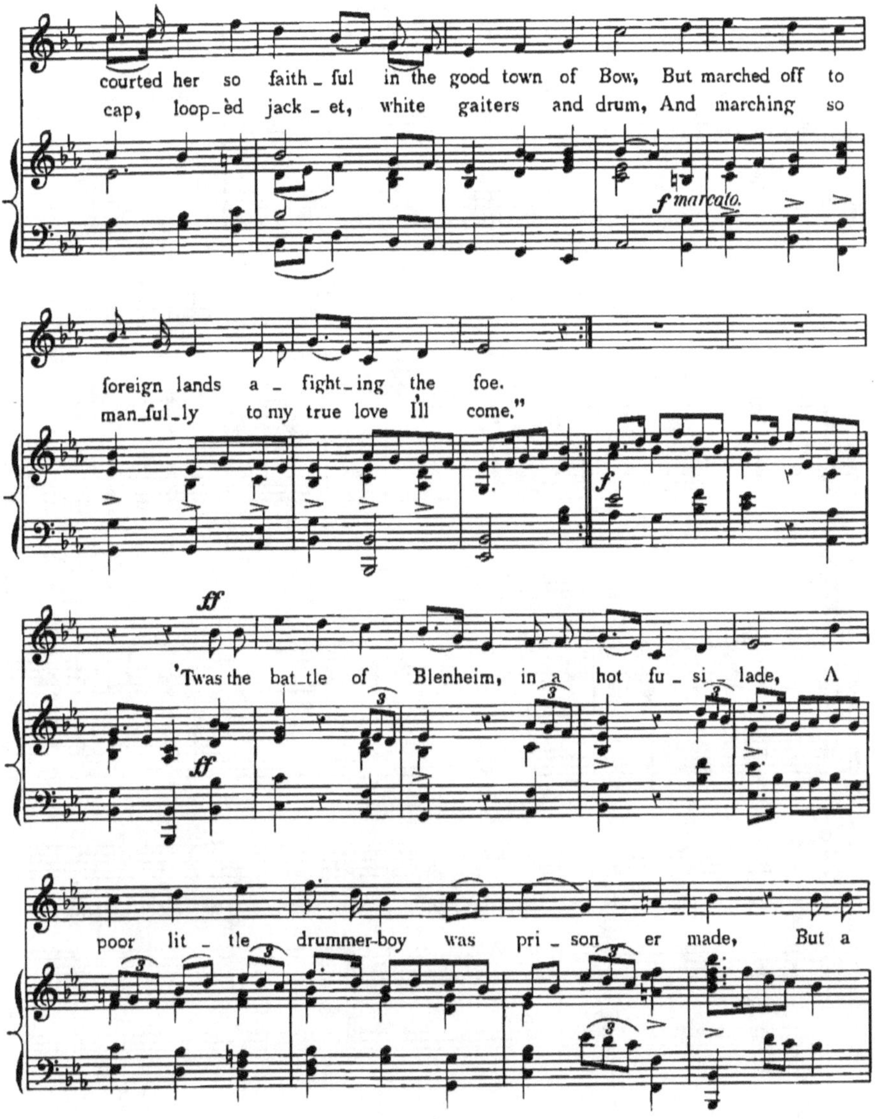
courted her so faith _ ful in the good town of Bow, But marched off to
cap, loop _ èd jack _ et, white gaiters and drum, And marching so
f marcato.
foreign lands a _ fight _ ing the foe.
man _ ful _ ly to my true love I'll come."
f
ff
'Twas the bat _ tle of Blenheim, in a hot fu _ si _ lade, A
ff
poor lit _ tle drummer-boy was pri _ son _ er made, But a

PRETTY POLLY OLIVER.

O pretty Polly Oliver, the pride of her sex,
The love of a grenadier her poor heart did vex;
He courted her so faithful in the good town of Bow,
But marched off to foreign lands a fighting the foe.

"I cannot rest single, nor false I'll not prove,
So I'll list for a drummer boy and follow my love,
Peak cap, loopèd jacket, white gaiters and drum,
And marching so manfully to my true love I'll come."

'Twas the battle of Blenheim, in a hot fusilade,
A poor little drummer boy was prisoner made,
But a brave grenadier fought his way thro' the foe,
And fifteen fierce Frenchmen together laid low.

He bore the boy tenderly in his arms as he swooned,
He opened his jacket for to search for a wound;
"O pretty Polly Oliver, my bravest, my bride,
Your true love shall nevermore be torn from your side."

The birds they sang joyously in that far foreign land,
The drums beat triumphantly with bugle and band,
Said Marlborough, "Queen Anne, and all England shall hear,
How I wed Polly Oliver to the brave grenadier."

HAROLD BOULTON.

The Three Ravens.

IX.

THE THREE RAVENS.

There were three ravens sat on a tree,
Down a down, a down, hey down;
They were as black as black might be,
With a down;
And one of them said to his mate,
"Where shall we our breakfast take?"
With a down, derry, derry derry down, down.

Oh! down, alas, in yon green field,
Down a down, a down, hey down;
A knight lies slain beneath his shield,
With a down.
His faithful hounds are at his feet,
So well do they their master keep,
With a down, derry, derry derry down, down.

His eager hawks about him fly,
Down a down, a down, hey down;
There's not a bird dare venture nigh,
With a down,
But down there came a fallow doe,
She was his love you well might know,
With a down, derry, derry derry down, down.

She lifted up his knightly head,
Down a down, a down, hey down;
She kissed his wounds that were so red,
With a down.
So tenderly her lord she bore.
Where he might rest for evermore,
With a down, derry, derry derry down, down.

She buried him before the Prime,
Down a down, a down, hey down;
She died herself ere Evensong time.
With a down.
Now every man pray God may send
Such hawks, such hounds, and such a friend,
With a down, derry, derry derry down, down.

OLD SONG.
(Edited by HAROLD BOULTON.)

The Happy Farmer.

(HAROLD BOULTON.)

X.

THE HAPPY FARMER.

As I was ploughing my father's field,
Across the hill came Marjorie;
The farmer's eldest son was I,
The miller's daughter she.
She greeted me kindly as homeward she hied,
I prayed she would linger and walk by my side,
"Come back, come back, come back," I cried,
"And follow the plough with me."

'Twas up the furrow and down the next,
Companion sweet, tripped Marjorie.
I ploughed the field with might and main,
Could labour lighter be?
But sweetest she looked in the sunset red,
With her little white hand on my good nag's head;
"Stay always here, my dear," I said,
"And follow the plough with me."

We've long been wed, and the farm's our own,
With cows, and sows, and horses three;
The happiest man alive am I,
The happiest mother she.
If sorrow and care for a moment divide,
I've a charm that will bring her at once to my side,
"Come back, come back, come back, my bride,
And follow the plough with me."

HAROLD BOULTON.

Where be Going?

XI.

WHERE BE GOING?

Cornish words traditional.
English words taken from various editions.

Old Cornish air contributed by Rev. S. Baring-Gould and arranged by Arthur Somervell.

CORNISH SONG.

"WHERE BE GOING?"

"Where be going to, dear little maiden,
  With your red rosy cheeks and your black curly hair?"
"I be going a milking, kind little man," she said,
"'Tis dabbling in the dew makes the milkmaids fair."

"Shall I go with you, dear little maiden,
  With your red rosy cheeks and your black curly hair?"
"With all my heart, my kind little man," she said,
"'Tis dabbling in the dew makes the milkmaids fair."

"Shall I wed you, dear little maiden,
  With your red rosy cheeks and your black curly hair?"
"With that I agree, my kind little man," she said,
"'Tis dabbling in the dew makes the milkmaids fair."

(Words taken from various editions.)

KÂN KERNIW.
PA LE ER EW WHY MOAZ.

Pa le er ew why moaz môz vean whêg,
Gen alaz thêg hagaz blèu melyn?
Mi a moaz a ha leath ba firra whêg,
A delkiow sevi gura muzi têg!

Ka ve moaz gan a why, môz vean whêg,
Gen alaz thêg hagaz blèu melyn?
Gen oll an collan sirra whêg,
A delkiow sevi gura muzi têg!

Pa le'r ew an Bew, môz vean whêg,
Gen alaz thêg hagaz blèu melyn?
En park an mow, ba firra whêg,
A delkiow sevi gura muzi têg!

TRADITIONAL.

Doun in yon Bank

(HAROLD BOULTON.)

XII.

DOUN IN YON BANK.

Doun in yon bank, where sings the merle early,
  Sits a puir lassie wha greets fit to dee;
Aye will she moan and sob fu' sairly,
  Watchin' the burnie rin doun to the sea.
    "My Jamie is fause and my heart it is broken, broken."

"I ken but ae lilt, I'll hear of nane ither,
  Near the wild wave I've sung it lang syne;
Weary saut sea, we'll croon it thegither,
  Maybe t'will comfort thy sorrow and mine.
    My Jamie is fause and my heart it is broken, broken."

HAROLD BOULTON.

Here's to Thy Health.

XIII.

HERE'S TO THY HEALTH.

Here's to thy health, my bonnie lass,
Guid night and joy be wi' thee;
I'll come nae mair to thy bower door,
To tell thee that I lo'e thee.
O dinna think, my pretty pink,
But I can live without thee;
I vow and sware, I dinna care,
How lang ye look about ye.

But far off fowl hae feathers rare,
And are until ye try them;
Though they seem fair, still have a care,
They may prove as bad as I am.
But at twel' at night, when the moon shines bright,
My dear, I'll come and see thee,
For the man that lo'es his mistress weel,
Nae travel maks him weary.

ROBERT BURNS.

O `She's Bonnie.

XIV.

OH SHE'S BONNIE!

№ 14.

Words Traditional.

Old Scottish Air arranged by
ARTHUR SOMERVELL.

Andante.

1. Gently blaw ye eastern breezes, Hide your piercing breath like store, An' cauld December frost that freezes, Frae the fair maid I adore.
2. Red's her cheek and sweet's her feature, Glancin' e'en like diamonds bright, Handsome shape, the choice o' nature, Wonder o' the day an night.

con espress.

Oh she's bonnie, bonnie, bonnie, Oh she's bonnie and sweet to see, Fair the bud an' bonnie blossom, Aye the blythe blink's

(J. H. C. & Co 10,327.)

OH! SHE'S BONNIE!

Gently blaw ye eastern breezes,
   Hide your piercing breath like store,
An' cauld December frost that freezes,
   Frae the fair maid I adore.

      Oh! she's bonnie, bonnie, bonnie,
         Oh! she's bonnie and sweet to see,
      Fair the bud an' bonnie blossom,
         Aye the blythe blink's in her e'e!

Frae winter's scoure, frae summer torment,
   Hoary mists that point the air,
Frae grief o' mind that aft does foment,
   Making life a dreary care.

      Oh! she's bonnie, etc.

For she's as the new blawn rose,
   That's nourish'd with the summer's sun;
Her smiles are like the sweet repose
   Man seeks when his last sand is run.

      Oh! she's bonnie, etc.

Red's her cheek, and sweet's her feature,
   Glancin' een like diamonds bright,
Handsome shape, the choice o' nature,
   Wonder o' the day and night.

      Oh! she's bonnie, etc.

If this bud and bonnie blossom,
   I could say 'twere only mine,
I'd plant it deep within my bosom,
   An' round my heart I'd it entwine.

      Oh! she's bonnie, etc.

                  TRADITIONAL.

Blink over the Burn.

(ROBERT ALLAN.)

XV.

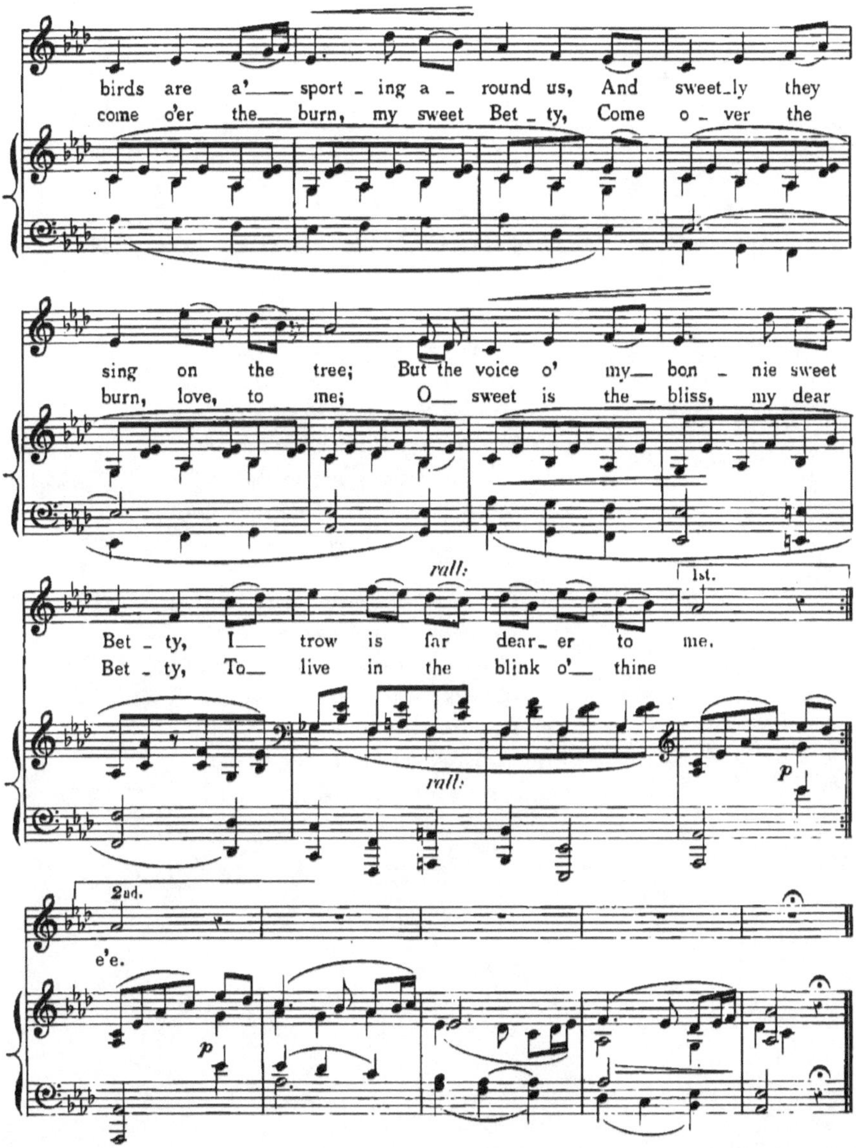
birds are a'— sport-ing a-round us, And sweet-ly they
come o'er the— burn, my sweet Bet-ty, Come o-ver the
sing on the tree; But the voice o' my— bon-nie sweet
burn, love, to me; O— sweet is the— bliss, my dear
Bet-ty, I— trow is far dear-er to me.
Bet-ty, To— live in the blink o'— thine
e'e.
rall:
1st.
2nd.
p

BLINK OVER THE BURN.

Blink over the burn, my sweet Betty,
    Blink over the burn, love, to me;
O lang ha'e I look'd, my dear Betty,
    To get but a blink o' thine e'e.
The birds are a' sporting around us,
    And sweetly they sing on the tree;
But the voice o' my bonnie sweet Betty,
    I trow, is far dearer to me.

The ringlets, my lovely young Betty,
    That wave o'er thy bonnie e'e-bree,
I'll twine wi' the flow'rs o' the mountain,
    That blossom sae sweetly, like thee.
Then come o'er the burn, my sweet Betty,
    Come over the burn, love, to me;
O sweet is the bliss, my dear Betty,
    To live in the blink o' thine e'e.

ROBERT ALLAN.

Scots wha hae.

(ROBERT BURNS.)

XVI.

SCOTS WHA HAE.

Scots wha hae wi' Wallace bled,
Scots wham Bruce hath aften led,
Welcome to your gory bed,
    Or to victorie!

Now's the day, and now's the hour,
See the front o' battle lour,
See approach proud Edward's power,—
    Chains and slaverie!

Wha wad be a traitor-knave?
Wha wad fill a coward's grave?
Wha 'sae base as be a slave?
    Let him turn and flee!

Wha for Scotland's king and law,
Freedom's sword will strongly draw,
Freeman stand or freeman fa'—
    Let him follow me!

By oppression's woes and pains,
By your sons in servile chains,
We will drain our dearest veins,
    But they shall be free!

Lay the proud usurpers low!
Tyrants fall in every foe!
Liberty's in every blow!
    Let us do or dee!

                    ROBERT BURNS.

Mary Jamieson.

XVII.

MARY JAMIESON.

N° 17.

Words Traditional.

Old Scottish Air arranged by ARTHUR SOMERVELL.

Adagio ma non troppo.

I hae lo'ed ye, Ma—ry Jamieson, As bride—groom ne'er lo'ed bride; The hours flew by, I

MARY JAMIESON.

I hae lo'ed ye, Mary Jamieson,
　As bridegroom ne'er lo'ed bride;
The hours flew by, I wistna how,
　When ye stood by my side.
Ye kent my heart was a' your ain,
　Mair lo'ed ye couldna be;
But loveless heart, and hameless love,
　Are a' ye left to me.

At the cuckoo's time o' comin',
　Ye were wi' me at the well;
At the swallow's time o' flittin',
　I stood there by mysel'.
But snaw upon the surging sea,
　Nor dew upon the flower,
Fleets not sae soon, fades not sae fast,
　As fleets love's little hour.

　　　　　　　　　TRADITIONAL.

Twine the Plaiden.

XVIII.

TWINE THE PLAIDEN.

O! I hae lost my silken snood,*
  That tied my hair sae yellow;
I've gi'en my heart to the lad I lo'ed,
  He was a gallant fellow.

    And twine it weel, my bonnie doo,
      And twine it weel, the plaiden;
    The lassie lost her silken snood,
      In pu'ing of the bracken.

He prais'd my een, sae bonnie blue,
  Sae lily-white my skin o',
And syne he pric'd my bonnie mou,
  And sware it was nae sin o'.

    And twine it weel, etc.

But he has left the lass he lo'ed,
  His ain true love forsaken;
Which gars me fair to greet the snood,
  I lost amang the bracken.

    And twine it weel, etc.

TRADITIONAL.

* The "Snood" was a riband for the hair, worn by unmarried women.

Will ye no come back again?
(LADY NAIRNE.)

XIX.

WILL YE NO COME BACK AGAIN?

No 19.

Words by
LADY NAIRNE.

Old Scottish Air arranged by
ARTHUR SOMERVELL.

Ro - yal Char - lie's now a - wa', Safe - ly owre the friend - ly main;
Hills he trode were a' his ain, And bed be - neath the birk - en - tree;

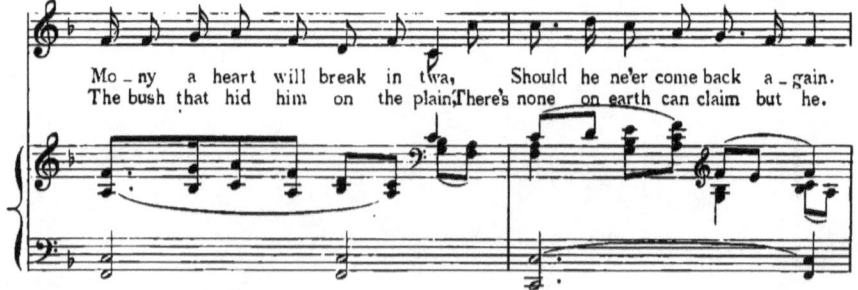

Mo - ny a heart will break in twa, Should he ne'er come back a - gain.
The bush that hid him on the plain, There's none on earth can claim but he.

*Published by arrangement with Messrs Paterson & Sons, Edinburgh.

(J. B. C. & Co 10,527.)

"WILL YE NO COME BACK AGAIN?"

Royal Charlie's now awa',
  Safely owre the friendly main;
Mony a heart will break in twa,
  Should he ne'er come back again.

    Will ye no come back again?
    Will ye no come back again?
    Better lo'ed ye canna be,
    Will ye no come back again?

Mony a traitor 'mang the Isles
  Brak' the band o' nature's law;
Mony a traitor, wi' his wiles,
  Sought to wear his life awa.

    Will ye no come back again? etc.

Ye trusted in your Hieland men,
  They trusted you, dear Charlie;
They kent your hiding in the glen,
  Death or exile braving.

    Will ye no come back again? etc.

We watched thee in the gloaming hour,
  We watched thee in the morning grey,
Tho' thirty thousand pounds they'd gie,
  Oh! there is none that would betray.

    Will ye no come back again? etc.

The hills he trode were a' his ain,
  And bed beneath the birken tree;
The bush that hid him on the plain,
  There's none on earth can claim but he.

    Will ye no come back again? etc.

Whene'er I hear the blackbird sing,
  Unto the e'ening sinkin' doun,
Or merle that mak's the woods to ring,
  To me they hae nae ither soun'!
    Than "Will ye no come back again?" etc.

Mony a gallant sodger fought,
  Mony a gallant chief did fa';
Death itself were dearly bought,
  A' for Scotland's king and law.

    Will ye no come back again? etc.

Sweet the lav'rock's note and lang,
  Liltin' wildly up the glen;
And aye to me he sings ae song,
  "Will ye no come back again?"

    Will ye no come back again? etc.

                        LADY NAIRNE.
                (With Traditional Verses added from time to time.)

In Yon Garden.

XX.

IN YON GARDEN.

№ 20.

Words Traditional.

Old Scottish Air arranged by
ARTHUR SOMERVELL.

In yon gar_den fine and gay,

Pick_ing lil_ies a' the day, Ga_thring flow'rs of il_ka hue, I

wist_na then what love could do. Where love is planted

(J. B. C. & C? 10,527.)

IN YON GARDEN.

In yon garden fine and gay,
Picking lilies a' the day,
Gath'ring flow'rs of ilka hue,
I wistna then what love could do.

Where love is planted there it grows,
It buds and blooms like any rose;
It has a sweet and pleasant smell,
No flow'r on earth can it excel.

I put my hand into the bush,
And thought the sweetest rose to find,
But prick'd my finger to the bone,
And left the sweetest rose behind.

      TRADITIONAL.

Were na My Heart Licht.

(LADY GRIZELL BAILLIE.)

XXI.

WERE NA MY HEART LICHT.

There was anes a may, and she lo'ed na men,
The biggit her bonnie bouir doun i' yon glen;
But now she cries, "Dule and a-well-a-day!
Come doun the green gate, and come here away."

When bonnie young Johnie cam ower the sea,
He said he saw naething sae bonnie as me;
He hecht me baith rings and monie braw things;
And were na my heart licht I wad dee.

He had a wee titty that lo'ed na me,
Because I was twice as bonnie as she;
She raised such a pother 'twixt him and his mother,
That were na my heart licht I wad dee.

The day it was set, and the bridal to be:
The wife took a dwam, and lay down to dee.
She main'd, and she grain'd, out o' dolour and pain,
Till he vow'd that he ne'er wad see me again.

His kin was for ane of a higher degree,
Said "What had he to do wi' the like of me?"
Albeit I was bonnie, I was na for Johnie,
And were na my heart licht I wad dee.

They said I had neither cow nor caff,
Nor dribbles o' drink rins through the draff,
Nor pickles o' meal rins through the mill-e'e;
And were na my heart licht I wad dee.

His titty she was baith wylie and slee,
She spied me as I cam ower the lea;
And then she ran in, and made a loud din;
Believe your ain e'en an ye trow na me.

His bonnet stood aye fou round on his brow,
His auld ane look'd aye as well as some's new;
But now he lets 't wear ony gate it will hing,
And casts himself dowie upon the corn bing.

And now he gaes drooping about the dykes,
And a' he daur do is to hund the tykes;
The live-lang nicht he ne'er steeks his e'e;
And were na my heart licht I wad dee.

Were I young for thee as I hae been,
We should hae been gallopin' doun on yon green,
And linkin' it on the lilie-white lea;
And wow gin I were but young for thee.

LADY GRIZEL-BAILLIE.

The Isle of the Heather

(M. MACLEOD.)

XXII.

THE ISLE OF THE HEATHER.

Chorus.—O isle of the heather, my heart longs for thee,
Like the salmon, the plover, the deer to be free,
Where by loch, sound and river, in green strath and glen,
Thrive the choicest of cattle, the bravest of men.

Our little grey Lewis has for all time stood forth,
The gem of the ocean, the pride of the north;
May the sun's guiding glory upon her be shed,
That her crops may have increase, her people be fed.
  Chorus.—O, isle of the heather, etc.

Dear isle of all others, a thousand times blest,
That bountiful nature has stored with its best,
'Tis there my devotion shall be till I die,
And Gaelic be spoken till ocean run dry.
  Chorus.—O, isle of the heather, etc.

There's a soft mist at dawn on the dark mountain brows,
While the light-hearted dairymaid sings to her cows,
They yield milk in plenty, beguiled by her strain,
And the rocks all around her repeat the refrain.
  Chorus.—O, isle of the heather, etc.

The cattle at gloaming-tide frisk in the dew,
While tunefully warbles the cheery cuckoo;
On the bough pipes the mavis, aloft the lark trills,
The lambs gamble gaily on grassy green hills.
  Chorus.—O, isle of the heather, etc.

No child of the island, but loves her to-day,
No creature would wish from her mountains to stray;
The birds that fly hither would bide evermore,
The fish love to throng by her sheltering shore.
  Chorus.—O, isle of the heather, etc.

Could age lose its weakness, and youth be my fee,
Alone and in freedom a shepherd I'd be;
A shealing I'd build 'mid the mountains on high,
Sweet milk and rich kebbuck my wants would supply.
  Chorus.—O, isle of the heather, etc.

But the fair isle of Lewis in most beauty is dressed,
When the sun sinks to rest in the ruddy north-west,
The herd from the rushes is gathering the kine,
Secure in the shealing, the young calves recline.
  Chorus.—O, isle of the heather, etc.

Of a long winter evening around the peat fire,
The youth learns the lore of his grey-headed sire,
The fisherman plies net and needle within;
The daughters card deftly, the mothers they spin.
  Chorus.—O, isle of the heather, etc.

Oh! fain 'mid the haunts of my boyhood I'd roam,
A-scaling the rocks to the bird's hidden home;
'Twas the thick gloom of Glasgow my happiness stole,
For the din of her hammers has deafened my soul.
  Chorus.—O, isle of the heather, etc.

Translated by HAROLD BOULTON.

EILEAN AN FHRAOICH

Fonn.—A chiall nach mise 'bha'n Eilean an Fhraoich!
  Nam fiadh, nam bradan, nam feadag, 's nan naosg!
  Nan lochan, nan òban, nan òsan 's nan caol—
  Eilean innis nam bò, 's àite-còmhnuidh nan laoch!

Tha Leòghas bheag riabhach,—bha i riamh 's an Taobh Tuath,—
Muir tràghaidh a's lionaidh 'g a h-iadhadh mu'n cuairt;
'N uair a dhèarrsas a' ghrian oirr' le fiaghladh 'o shuas
Bheir i fàs air gach sìol air son biadh dha'n an t-sluagh.
  Fonn.—A chiall nach mise 'bha'n Eilean an Fhraoich! etc.

An t-Eilean ro mhaiseach, gur pailt ann am biadh;
'Se Eilean a's àillt' air'n do dhèallraich a' ghrian;
'Se Eilean mo ghràidh-s' e, bbs 'Ghàidhlig ann riamh;
'S cha 'n fhalbh i gu bràth gus an tràigh an cuan siar!
  Fonn.—A chiall nach mise 'bha'n Eilean an Fhraoich! etc.

'N àm èiridh na gréine air a shlèibhtibh bidh ceò,
Bidh 'bhanarach ghuanach 's a' bhuarach 'n a dòrn,
Ri gabhail a duanaig 's i 'g uallach nam bò,
'S mac-talla nan creag ri toirt freagairt d'a ceòl.
  Fonn.—A chiall nach mise' bha'n Eilean an Fhraoich! etc.

Air feasgar an t-Sàmhraidh bidh sunnd air gach spréidh;
Bidh 'chuthag a's fonn oirr' ri òran di fèin;
Bidh uiseag air lòn agus smeòrach air géig,
'S air cnuic ghlas a's lòintean uain òga ri leum.
  Fonn.—A chiall nach mise' bha'n Eilean an Fhraoich! etc.

Gach duine 'bha riamh ann bha ciatamh ac' dhà,
Gach ainmhidh air sliabh ann, cha'n iarr às gu bràth;
Gach eun 'thèid air giath ann bu mhiann leis ann tàmh;
'S bu mhiann le gach iasg a bhi 'cliathadh ri'thràigh.
  Fonn.—A chiall nach mise 'bha'n Eilean an Fhraoich! etc.

Na 'm faighinn mo dhùrachd 's e 'luiginn bhi òg,
'S gun ghnothach aig aois rium fhad 's a dh 'fhaodainn bhi beò;
Bhi 'n am bhuachaill 'air àiridh fo shàil nam beann mòr'
Far am faighinn an càis' 's bainne blàth air son òl.
  Fonn.—A chiall nach mise 'bha'n Eilean an Fhraoich! etc.

Cha 'n fhacas air talamh leam sealladh is bòidhch'
Na 'ghrian a' dol sios air taobh siar Eilean Leòghais:
'N crodh-laoidh anns an luachair, 's am buachaill 'n an tòir,
'G ac tional gu àiridh le àl de laoidh òg.
  Fonn.—A chiall nach mise 'bha'n Eilean an Fhraoich! etc.

Air feasgar a' gheamhraidh thèid tionndadh gu gnìomh
Ri toirt eòlais do chloinn bidh gach seann duine liath;
Gach iasgair le 'shoathbaìd ri càradh a lìon,
Gach nighean ri càrdadh 's a màthair ri sniomh.
  Fonn.—A chiall nach mise 'bha'n Eilean an Fhraoich! etc.

B'e mo mhiann bhi 's na badain 's 'na chleachd mi bhi òg,
Ri direadh nan creag anns an neadaich na h-eòin;
O' n thàinig mi 'Ghlaschu tha m' aigneadh fo bhròn,
'S mi 'cell mo chuid clàistneachd le glagrich nan òrd.
  Fonn.—A chiall nach mise 'bha'n Eilean an Fhraoich!
  Nam fiadh, nam bradan, nam feadag, 's nan naosg—!
  Nan lochan, nan òban, nan òsan 's nan caol—
  Eilean innis nam bò, 's àite-còmhnuidh nan laoch!

MURDOCH MACLEOD.

The Mackintosh's Lament.

(Translated by HAROLD BOULTON.)

XXIII.

THE MACKINTOSH'S LAMENT.
(CUMHA MHIC-AN-TOISICH.)

N° 23.

Gaelic Words Traditional.
Translated from the Gaelic by
Harold Boulton.

Old Highland Air arranged by
Arthur Somervell.

Lies clan Chattan's glory! Cursed thy breed, thou treacherous steed, That failed the rider at his need! Black thy colour, Black the deed! and black thy name in story!

THE MACKINTOSH'S LAMENT.

Grief of heart! heart of grief!
Fallen is the warrior chief;
Fallen like a summer leaf,
Lies Clan Chattan's glory!

Cursed thy breed, thou treacherous steed,
That failed the rider at his need!
Black thy colour, black the deed,
Black thy name in story.

Bitter doom! hapless bride,
Newly parted from his side,
When my true love, stricken sore,
Met his death ill-fated!

Wine for wedding feast prepared,
Friends at wake and funeral shared;
Sorrow, sorrow, evermore!
The bride must mourn unmated.

HAROLD BOULTON.

This lament is supposed to have been composed by the bride of a chief of the Clan Chattan who met his death by a fall from his horse on returning from his wedding.

CUMHA MHIC-AN-TOISICH.

Thog iad thu! leag iad thu!
Ceud nan creach, thog iad thu!
Thog iad thu, laoigh, leag iad thu!
Dheagh a Mhic-an-Toisich.

Leag an t-each dubh, cionnan thu!
Leag an t-each dubh, cionnan thu!
Leag an t-each dubh, cionnan thu!
Am bealach garbh a' ghàraidh.

'S truagh nach robh mis' an sin,
'S truagh nach robh mis' an sin,
'S truagh nach robh mi ann an sin
Is bheirinn air an làimh ort.

'M fion a bha air son do bhainnse,
'M fion a bha air son do bhainnse,
Dh' òladh air do fhairir e,
Dheagh a Mhic-an-Toisich.

TRADITIONAL.

The Opening of the Key.

(HAROLD BOULTON.)

XXIV.

THE OPENING OF THE KEY.

No. 24.

(AGORIAD Y CYWAIR)

English words by HAROLD BOULTON.
Welsh simile by G. M. PROBERT.

Old Welsh air arranged by
ARTHUR SOMERVELL.

(J. B. C. & Co. 10,627.)

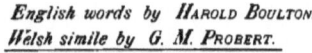

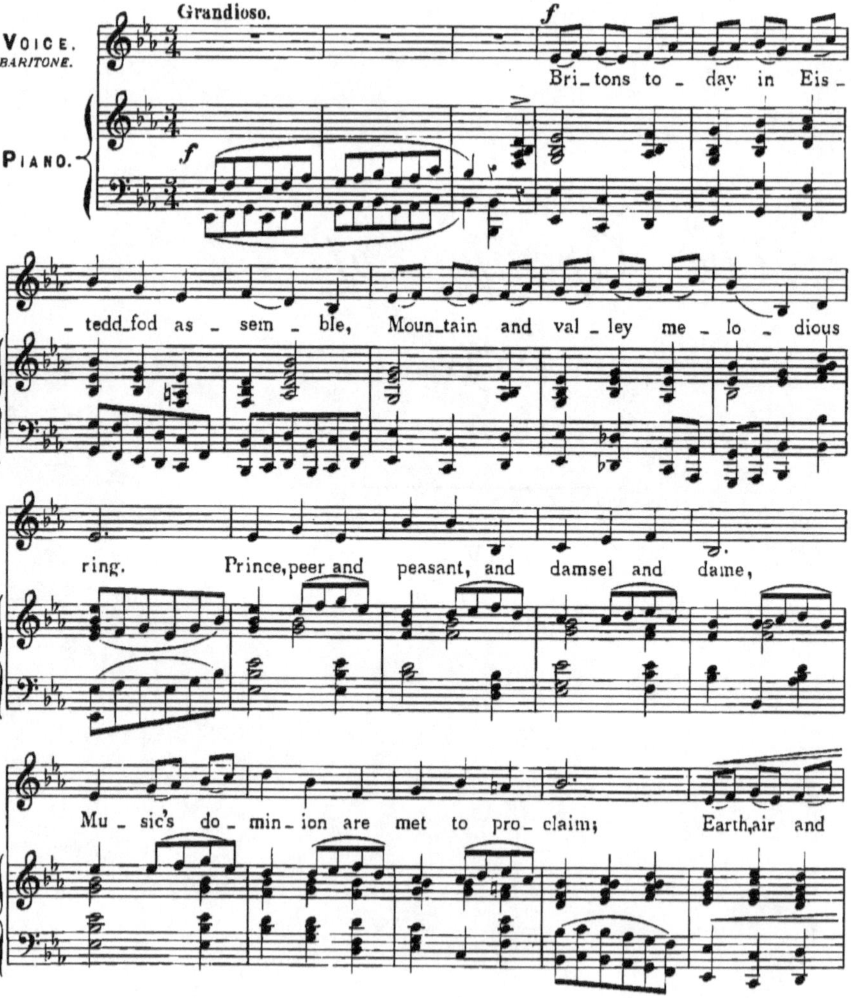

THE OPENING OF THE KEY.

Britons to-day in Eisteddfod assemble,
  Mountain and Valley melodious ring;
    Prince, peer and peasant, and damsel and dame
    Music's dominion are met to proclaim,
Earth, air and sea, with their symphony tremble,
  Heaven's arches answer "The Minstrel is King."

Let loves and battles of Cymry departed,
  Flash, bards inspired, like a flame from your string;
    Let voice and harp in Pennillion blend,
    Let skilful triad your wisdom commend.
Winner or loser contend open-hearted,
  Power to your prowess, the Minstrel is King.

Summon the victor, and gird him with glory,
  The chair and the crown for his ornament bring;
    Three times with challenge the sword hold on high,
    Three times tumultuous let all men reply:
Heights of Plinlimmon, and Snowdon the hoary,
  Ye shall be witness, the Minstrel is King.

                  HAROLD BOULTON.

AGORIAD Y CYWAIR.

Dyma brif-wyl gwlad ein tadau,
Gwlad a chryd yr Eisteddfodau;
Gwlad y Bardd a'i hoff ddefodau,
  Gwyliau hen ein Gwalia Wen.
Gwreng a boneddwr sydd yma'n gytûn,
Awen fawrygir a'i pherchen yr un.
Enill "Cadair" yr Eisteddfod!
Dyna gamp a dyna brif-nod
Ddenodd feirdd pob oes a chyfnod;
  Tystia'r oll, "Y Bardd sy'n ben."

Cana'r beirdd am ddewrion Cymru,
Am wladgarwch a gwrhydri,
Ac am ereill fu'n rhagori.
  Mebion hoff i gân a llên.
"Deuwch a'r 'Gadair' i'r gŵr bia'r dydd,
Deuwch a'r delyn a chlêdd Cymru fydd."
"A oes heddwch?" clywch y geiriau;
"Heddwch," etyb myrdd o leisiau,
Adsain ddaw yn ol o'r creigiau,
  Tystia'r oll, "Y Bardd sy'n ben."

                  G. M. PROBERT.

N.B.—The Welsh words (5th and 6th lines excepted) have been written with a syllable to every semiquaver, instead of a syllable to two semiquavers as in the English words.

The Slender Boy.

(HAROLD BOULTON.)

XXV.

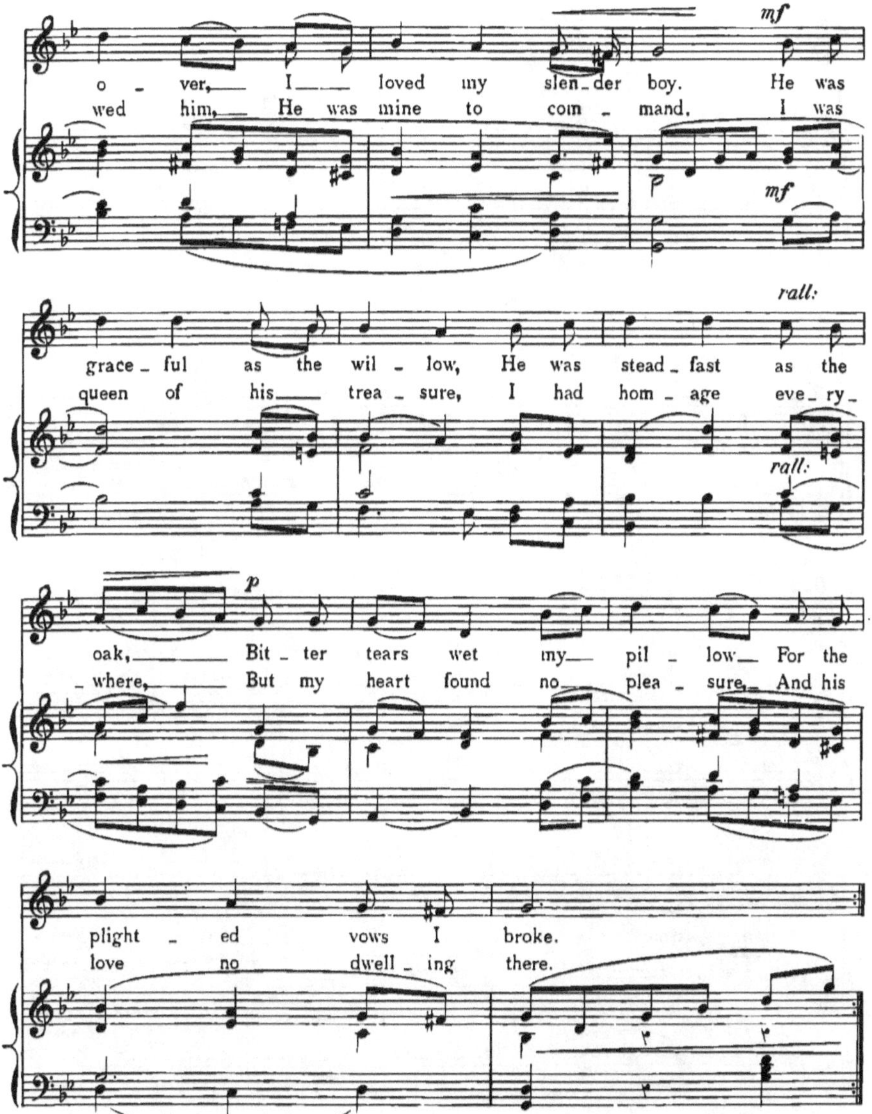
mf
o - ver, I loved my slen - der boy. He was
wed him, He was mine to com - mand. I was
mf
rall:
grace - ful as the wil - low, He was stead - fast as the
queen of his trea - sure, I had hom - age eve - ry -
rall:
p
oak, Bit - ter tears wet my pil - low For the
- where, But my heart found no plea - sure, And his
plight - ed vows I broke.
love no dwell - ing there.

*The pronunciation of this word in Welsh is nearer in the vowel sounds to the English ow than to aw.

THE SLENDER BOY.

In the fair Vale of Clwyd in the days of my joy,
Ere the primrose was over, I loved my slender boy,
He was graceful as the willow, he was steadfast as the oak,
Bitter tears wet my pillow for the plighted vows I broke.

Brave Sir David came wooing with houses and land;
Though I cared not, I wed him, he was mine to command,
I was queen of his treasure, I had homage everywhere,
But my heart found no pleasure, and his love no dwelling there.

With the spring comes the primrose to brighten Plas Draw,*
But my life knows no springtime in the Vale of Clwyd now.
Oh! a snare is ambition, foolish woman to destroy,
All in vain my contrition, for I love my slender boy!

HAROLD BOULTON.

* The pronunciation of this word in Welsh is nearer in the vowel sounds to the English *o, w,* than to *a, w.*

Y BACHGEN MAIN.

Pan yn ieuangc yn y Dyffryn,
Ysgafn galon dan fy mron,
Heb un gofid yn fy mlino,
Canu wnawn o hyd yn llon;
Cariad ddaeth a'i saethau treiddiol,
'Nelodd ataf, clwyfodd fi;
Clwyf dolurus, clwyf pleserus
Oedd y clwyf a gefais i.

Yn y Gwanwyn daeth y blodau,
Yn yr Haf daeth mwy o'r rhai'n,
Yn yr Hydref daeth fy nghariad,
Cariad oedd y Bachgen Main;
Teg ei wyneb, dewr ei galon,
Ymfalchio ynwyf wnai;
O! na fuaswn inau'n ffyddlon
I fy Machgen Main difai.

Daeth Syr Dafydd gyda'i gyfoeth,
Minau gludwyd gyda'r ffrwd;
Bu'n edifar genyf ganwaith,
'Nawr 'rwy'n medi'r chwerw gnwd;
Er i'm gerddi dyfu'r lili,
Yn fy nghalon tyf y drain;
Er holl drysor gwych Syr Dafydd,
Caru 'rwyf y Bachgen Main.

G. M. PROBERT.

All Through the Night.

(HAROLD BOULTON.)

XXVI.

ALL THROUGH THE NIGHT.

Sleep my love and peace attend thee,
  All through the night;
Guardian angels God will lend thee,
  All through the night;
Soft the drowsy hours are creeping,
Hill and dale in slumber steeping,
Love alone his watch is keeping—
  All through the night.

Though I roam a minstrel lonely,
  All through the night;
My true harp shall praise thee only,
  All through the night;
Love's young dream, alas, is over,
Yet my strains of love shall hover
Near the presence of my lover,
  All through the night.

Hark! A solemn bell is ringing,
  Clear through the night;
Thou my love art heavenward winging,
  Home through the night;
Earthly dust from off thee shaken,
Soul immortal thou shalt waken,
With thy last dim journey taken
  Home through the night.

HAROLD BOULTON.

AR HYD Y NÔS.

Cwsg fy mûn, a hedd fo'th weinydd,
  Ar hyd y nos.
Engyl wyliant dy obenydd,
  Ar hyd y nos.
Tra y treigla'r oriau meithion,
Tra yr hepia natur weithion,
Serch sy'n effro a'i obeithion,
  Ar hyd y nos.

Er im' grwydro fel un annghall,
  Ar hyd y nos.
Ni wnai'm telyn foli arall,
  Ar hyd y nos.
Serch fu'n llunio llawen fwriad;
Treulio oriau gyda'i gariad,
Ond nid dyna fu fy mhrofiad
  Ar hyd y nos.

Clywch! mae cloch yn trymaidd seinio,
  Drwy'r ddistaw nos;
Fry mae'm cariad wedi hwylio,
  Drwy'r dywell nos;
Ond 'rol ysgwyd llwch daearol
Oddiwrthyt, O anfarwol!
Gorphwys gai ar serch tragwyddol,
  Mewn nef heb nos.

G. M. PROBERT.

The Dimpled Cheek.

XXVII.

THE DIMPLED CHEEK.

Thy dimpled cheek and sweet lovely mien,
Fill with delight every youth on the green;
Roses and lilies have lent their soft shade
To make thee more fair than any fair maid.

Oh! how I love thee—alas but in vain,
Thou art betrothed to a wealthier swain;
Still I adore thee—though thus I'm repaid,
For thou art more fair than any fair maid.

TRADITIONAL.

TWLL YN EI BOCH.

Prydferth ei hosgo, twll yn ei boch,
Dau lygad siriol, a dwy wefus goch;
Llangciau wirionent pan welent y fûn;
Pa ryfedd i'm syrthio mewn cariad fy hun?

O! fel ei carwn, ond gwastraff ar serch,—
Cyfoeth â'i swynion a hudodd y ferch;
Er iddi fy nhwyllo bydd byth yn fy mryd;
Pa ryfedd, 'does debyg i hon yn y byd!

G. M. PROBERT.

By the Waters of Babylon.

(Adapted by ARTHUR SOMERVELL.)

XXVIII.

BY THE WATERS OF BABYLON.

By the waters of Babylon we sat down and wept,
When we remembered Zion:
And as for our harps we hanged them up
On the willows that were therein.

For they that led us away captive
Required of us a song,
And they that wasted us required of us mirth,
"Sing us one of the songs of Zion."

How shall we sing the Lord's song
In a strange land?
Oh! if I forget thee, O Jerusalem,
Let my right hand forget her cunning.

If I do not remember thee,
Let my tongue cleave to the roof of my mouth,
Yea, if I prefer not Jerusalem,
Above my chief joy.

Remember the children of Edom,
O Lord, in the day of Jerusalem,
Who said "Let us raze the walls thereof,
Even unto the ground."

O daughter of Babylon, wasted with misery,
Happy the man that avengeth us,
Yea, blest shall he be that taketh thy little ones
And dasheth them against the ground!

Words selected from Psalm cxxxvii, by
ARTHUR SOMERVELL.

WRTH AFONYDD BABILON.

1 Wrth a-	fonydd Babilon, eistedd-	asom a wylâsom pan	feddyliâsom am	Sion :	Ar yr
2 Canys	yno gofynodd y	rhai a'n caethiwàsent i	ni ganu	càn :	a'r
3 Pa	fodd y cànwn gerdd yr	Arglwydd mewn	gwlad lle'r y'm yn	ddieithr?	Os
4	Glyned fy nhâfod with	daflod fy ngênau	oni choôfiaf	di ;	Oni
5	Cofia Arglwydd, blant	Edom yn	nydd Jerûsa-	lem ,	y
6 O	ferch Babilon a an-	rheithir ;	gwyn fyd yr ûn a'n di-	ala ,	Gwyn ei

helyg, o'u mewn, crog-	asom ein telynau; ar yr	helyg crogâsom hwynt	yno.	
rhai a'n hanreithâsant la-	wenydd, gan ddwêyd,	"Conweh i ni ganiadau	Sion."	
gwnaf dy anghôfio Jer-	usalem, an-	aghofied fy nehëulaw	ganu.	
chodaf dydl O Jer-	usalèm, gor-	uwch fy llawèuydd	penaf.	
rhai a ddy-wedent, " Dy-	noethweh hi : dy-	noethwch hi byd ei	sylfaen.	
fyd a gyuôra ac	a darâwo dy rai	bach; dy rai bâch wrth y	moini.	

TREFNWYD GAN G. M. PROBERT.

D.S.—Mae y bànau uchod yn cyfateh i fânau y gerddoriaeth; ac mae yr 1 uwchben sill acceuol yn dynodi hauer y'bân. Ni fydd un anhawsder i gerddor profiadol briodi y geirau a'r gerddoriaeth ond dylin neu adael allan nodau fel ho galwad.

Gwenllian.

(HAROLD BOULTON.)

XXIX.

GWENLLIAN.

No. 29.

Welsh Words written by
N. Bennett (Trefnant.)
English Translation by Harold Boulton

Old Welsh Air arranged by
Arthur Somervell

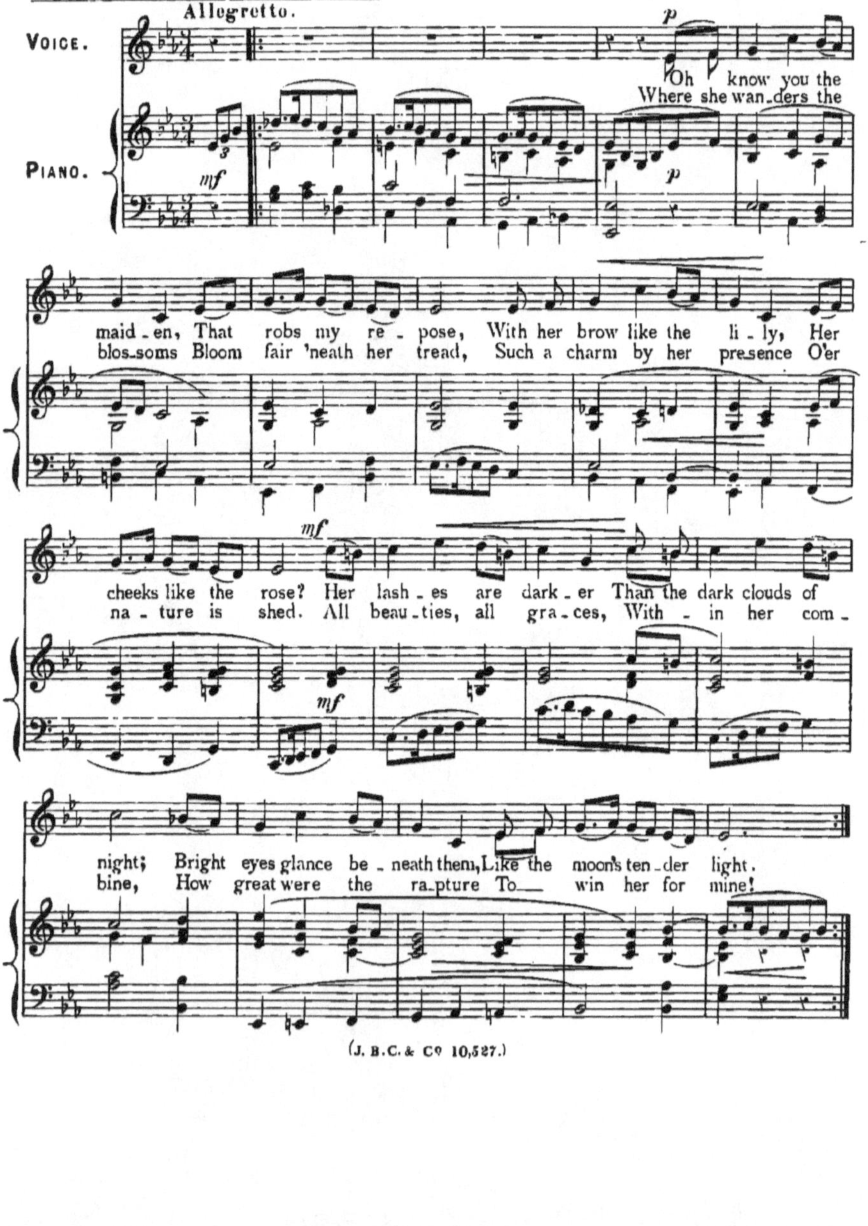
Allegretto.
Voice.
Piano.
p
mf
Oh know you the maid - en, That robs my re - pose, With her brow like the li - ly, Her cheeks like the rose? Her lash - es are dark - er Than the dark clouds of night; Bright eyes glance be - neath them, Like the moon's ten - der light.
Where she wan - ders the blos - soms Bloom fair 'neath her tread, Such a charm by her pre - sence O'er na - ture is shed. All beau - ties, all gra - ces, With - in her com - bine, How great were the ra - pture To win her for mine!

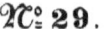

GWENLLIAN.

Oh, know you the maiden
  That robs my repose,
With her brow like the lily,
  Her cheeks like the rose?
Her lashes are darker
  Than the dark clouds of night,
Bright eyes glance beneath them,
  Like the moon's tender light.

Where she wanders the blossoms
  Bloom fair 'neath her tread,
Such a charm by her presence
  'Oer nature is shed.
All beauties, all graces,
  Within her combine;
How great were the rapture
  To win her for mine.

Oh, know you the maiden
  Of maidens most dear?
'Tis Gwenllian they call her,
  'Tis her I revere.
When an angel from heaven
  Came down among men,
They spared us the best one,
  And called her name GWEN!

Translated from the Welsh by
HAROLD BOULTON.

GWENLLIAN.

Adwaenoch chwi'r ferch ieuanc—
  Y feinwen siriol dlos,
Sy' a'r bochau gwynion gwridgoch
  A gywilyddia'r rhôs;
Ei haeliau main y'nt ddûach
  Na'r cymyl duon erch,
A'r llygaid sydd o danynt
  Belydra swynol serch.

P'le sang, cain flodau dardda
  Yn ôl ei bychan droed,
Ei gwên adlona'm natur—
  Ei bath ni bu erioed!
Y mae pob rhyw ragoriaeth
  Yn cydgwrdd ynddi hi—
Mae'n oll ellid ddymuno,
  A phob peth yw i mi.

Os gwelsoch chwi'r fath eneth—
  'Does modd a methu'r gû—
Gwenllian yw ei henw,
  A'm cariad ydyw hi;
Nid oes un fwy angylaidd
  O fewn y nefoedd wèn,
Ac ar y ddaear lydan
  'Does debyg i fy Ngwen!

N. BENNETT. (Trefnant.)

Jenny's Mantle.
(HAROLD BOULTON.)

XXX.

One kind smile to win be-fore they came to Mold. First the hood she
Not one fea-ture of her face could he be-hold. Now her hood she
clos-er tied, Then a lit-tle drew a-side, Ne-ver did maid-en fair
clos-er tied, Quiv-'ring eye and lip to hide, De-spe-rate, doubt-ful yet,
tease a lo-ver more; When it slipp'd a lit-tle down, Jen-ny tied it
Rich-ard swore a vow. "By the bones of all the dead, By the snow on
with a frown, Oh! that cru-el cloak that Jen-ny O-wen wore.
Snow-don's head, One last chance I'll try to win or lose her

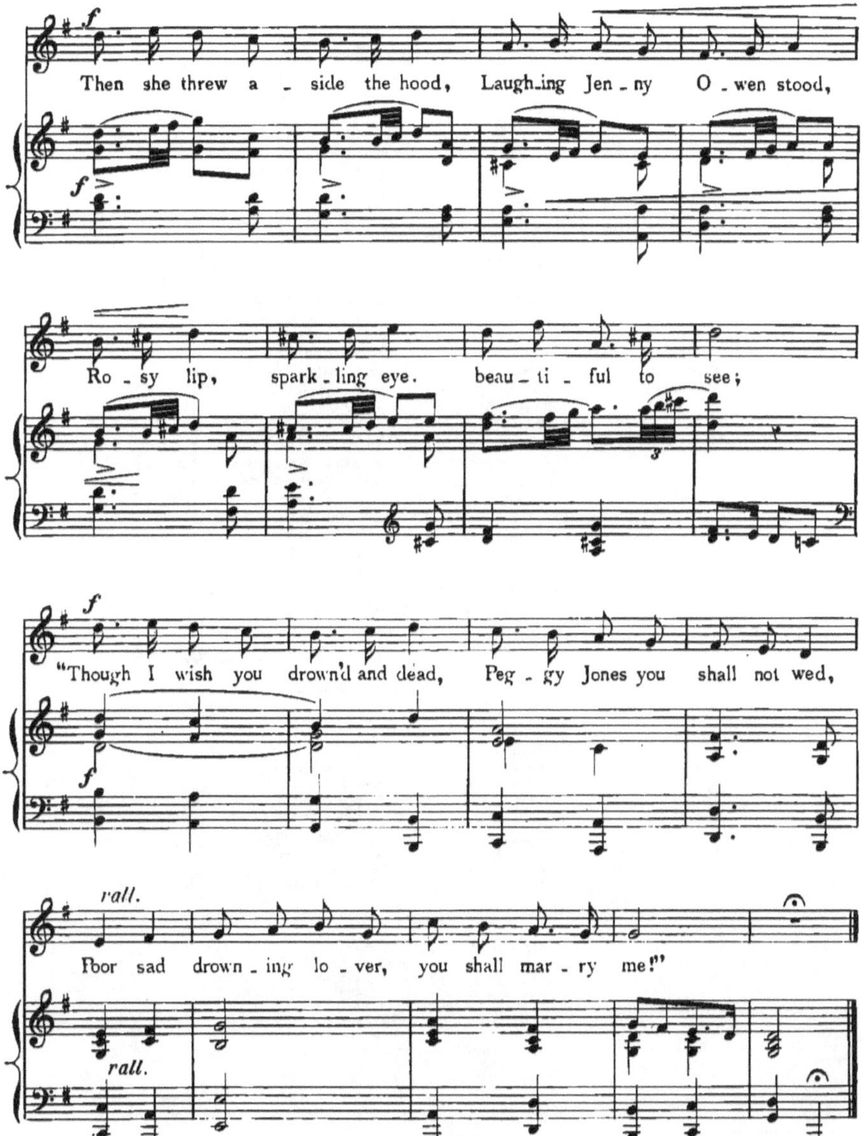
f
Then she threw a - side the hood, Laugh-ing Jen - ny O - wen stood,
Ro - sy lip, spark - ling eye. beau - ti - ful to see;
"Though I wish you drown'd and dead, Peg - gy Jones you shall not wed,
rall.
Poor sad drown - ing lo - ver, you shall mar - ry me!"

JENNY'S MANTLE.

Oh the long red cloak with a hood Jenny Owen wore,
    Bright-eyed Jenny from the farm beyond the fold;
Oh the love-lorn pain in his heart Richard Powell bore,
    One kind smile to win before they came to Mold.
        First the hood she closer tied,
        Then a little drew aside,
Never did maiden fair tease a lover more;
        When it slipped a little down,
        Then she tied it with a frown,
Oh that cruel cloak that Jenny Owen wore!

Oh the tender words, as they walked, Richard Powell said,
    A cunning tongue he had, like all the men of Mold;
But 'twas all in vain—no sign Jenny Owen made,
    Not one feature of her face could he behold.
        Now her hood she closer tied,
        Quivering eye and lip to hide,
Desperate, doubtful yet, Richard swore a vow:
        "By the bones of all the dead,
        By the snow on Snowdon's head,
One last chance I'll try to win or lose her now."

"'Tis a parting word you must now, Jenny Owen, take,
    No more time you have to treat me as of old,
For in Alyn's Stream I'll get drowned for your cruel sake,
    Or wed fat Peggy Jones, the ugliest in Mold."
        Then she threw aside the hood,
        Laughing, Jenny Owen stood,
Rosy lip, sparkling eye, beautiful to see:
        "Though I wish you drowned and dead,
        Peggy Jones you shall not wed,
Poor sad drowning lover, you shall marry me!"

                      HAROLD BOULTON.

MANTELL SIANI.

O! y fantell fain gyda hŵd a wisgai Siani Wyn,
Siani lygaid siriol, Siani Fotty'r Bryn;
O! y cur a'r cariad o fewn i fynwes un a fu,
Disgwyl gwên dros wefus goch y goegen gu!
    Clymu'r hŵd nes cuddio'i phryd,
    Yna datod fymryn byd,
Dyna'r fel denai'r fûn galon Deio'r Glyn;
    Pan y llithrai'r hŵd naill du,
    Gwgus glymai'r hoeden hi;
O! y fantell atgas wisgai Siani Wyn.

Accompaniment of last English verse for following:

O! y duedd dyner yn nghalon Dei i sisial serch
Swynai galon Siani, Siani gyndyn ferch;
O! y gynhen gyfrwys a godid gan y wamal fûn,
Dim ond dichell merch i enill cariad dyn!
    Darfu 'mynedd Deio'r Glyn,
    Geiriau garw,—Siani'n syn:
"Priodi wnaf Pegws Jones os na 'tebi di."
    Ymaith aeth yr hŵd yn syth—
    "Ni chai briodi Pegws byth."
"O! mae dynion am y dyla, coeliwch fi."

                      G. M. PROBERT.

Gwilym and Ellen.

XXXI.

GWILYM AND ELLEN.

(Written according to Parry by one Gwilym Davydd, himself the Gwilym of the song.)

Poor Ellen loved Gwilym, but loved him in vain,
He scoffed at her passion, and laughed at her pain;
The rose on her cheek once so blooming and fair,
Is now washed away by sorrow's sad tear.
One night thus she sang 'neath a tree in the grove,
" Alas hapless Ellen's a victim to love."

Thus sang in the midnight the sorrowful maid,
And wandered distraught through the dark forest glade,
Till weary with weeping she sank on the ground,
And lifeless at daybreak poor Ellen was found.
Too late came young Gwilym, contrition to prove,
There lay hapless Ellen, a victim to love.

Old words adapted by
HAROLD BOULTON.

GWILYM AC ELEN.

'R oedd Elen yn caru a chariad oedd bur,
Ond Gwilym a wawdiai ei dolur a'i chûr,
Diflanodd y rhosyn a liwiai ei grudd,
Fe'i golchwyd ef ymaith gan ddagrau y brudd;
Un noson fe ganai yn nghysgod y llwyn,
" Mae Elen yn aberth i gariad a'i swyn."

Ac felly y canai'n gwynfanus trwy'r nos,
Tra'n crwydro'n orphwyllog draws llwybrau y rhôs;
Ond blinder ei chalon a'i llêthodd i'r llawr,
Yn farw ca'dd Gwilym y fûn gyda'r wawr;
Rhy hwyr oedd ei ofid, rhy hwyr er ei mhwyn!
'Roedd Elen yn aberth i gariad a'i swyn.

G. M. PROBERT.

The Mistletoe.

(HAROLD BOULTON.)

XXXII.

THE MISTLETOE.

(CNOT Y COED.)

Nº 32.

English words by HAROLD BOULTON.
Welsh simile by G. M. PROBERT.

Old Welsh air arranged by
ARTHUR SOMERVELL.

THE MISTLETOE.

When winter fires glow warm and red,
    And mistletoe hangs on beam,
Then man and maid the dance should tread,
    With those they dearest deem.
        Nay, nay, Heyday!
Love has no such rule,
    For though my heart for someone burns,
That one to me is cool,
    For though my heart for someone burns,
That one is cool.

When heart of youth, with love elate,
    Melodious longs to sing,
Then surely each may choose a mate,
    Like birds that build in spring.
        Nay, nay, Heyday!
Love's not kind nor true,
    There's ever one must wear the rose,
And one must bear the rue,
    There's ever one must wear the rose,
And one the rue.

                HAROLD BOULTON.

CNOT Y COED.

Pan siriol dân rydd wrês hin oer,
    A'r uchelwydd grôg wrth y mûr,
Pryd hyny dawns y mab a'r ferch
    Sy'n caru a chariad pûr:
        Na, na, O na!
Serch heb reol sydd,
    Can's er im' garu un yn fawr,
Yr un i mi ni fydd;
    Can's er im' garu un yn fawr
I mi ni fydd.

Pan fo i'r galon drwy rym serch
    Hiraethu am ganu'n fwyn,
Ceir dewis cymhar, goeliaf fi,
    Mal adar yn y llwyn:
        Na, na, O na!
Serch sydd groes ei raen,
    Y'n wastad gwisga un y rhôs,
Tra arall ddwg y ddraen;
    Y'n wastad gwisga un y rhôs,
Ac un y ddraen.

                G. M. PROBERT.

The Melody of May.
(HAROLD BOULTON.)

XXXIII.

MELODY OF MAY.

(MWYNEN MAI.)

English words by HAROLD BOULTON.
Welsh simile by G. M. PROBERT.

Old Welsh air arranged by
ARTHUR SOMERVELL.

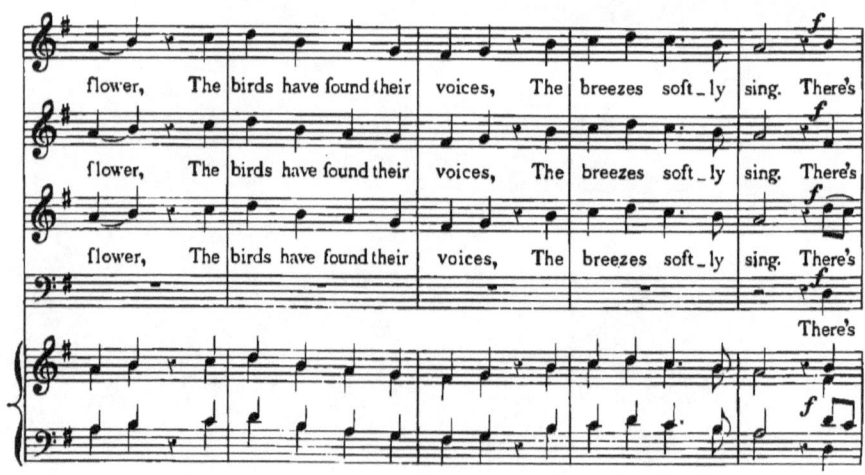

(J.B.C. & Co. 10,527.)

THE MELODY OF MAY.

No more the frost has power
To pinch the new-born flower,
   The birds have found their voices,
      The breezes softly sing.
There's music on the mountain,
There's music in the fountain,
   Creation all rejoices,
      So welcome is the spring.

The tribe of pale primroses,
That in yon dingle dozes,
   Wake up in coats of yellow
      To celebrate the spring;
The bluebells of the valley
Their brave battalions rally,
   Each nodding to its fellow,
      A happy chime they ring.

Then tread a measure merry,
Sweet maid with lips of cherry,
   And eyes of blue entrancing,
      Ye harpers tune your string;
In jig and morris mingle,
Till feet and pulses tingle,
   With feasting and with dancing
      We'll welcome in the spring.

                  HAROLD BOULTON.

MWYNEN MAI.

Nis gall y Gauaf oerwyn
Garcharu blodau'r Gwanwyn,
   Mae'nt hwy a'r mwyn delorion
      Yn canu ceingciau fyrdd;
Deffroi mae hynawa Anian
'R ol tymhor hir o hepian,
   A gwysia'r holl gerddorion
      I gwrdd a'r Gwanwyn gwyrdd.

Fe ddeffry'r briall melyn,
Sy'n cysgu dan y celyn,
   I ddathlu'r Gwanwyn newydd,
      Mewn gwisgoedd harddaf liw;
Ymgryma'r clychau gleision
Yn foesgar i'w cyfeillion,
   Tra'n chwareu gyda'u gilydd
      Groesawus gerddi gwiw.

Gan hyny troediwn ninau
Hen fesur gyda'r tánau,
   Pan "Mwynen Mai" chwareuant
      Ar grwth a thelyn fwyn;
Mewn ysgafn ddawns ymgymysg
Y lluaws llawen hydlysg,
   Yr oll mewn gwledd groesawant
      Y Gwanwyn pêr ei swyn.

                  G. M. PROBERT.

Dream of Little Rhys
(HAROLD BOULTON.)

XXXIV.

DREAM OF LITTLE RHYS.

(BREUDDWYD RHYSYN BACH.)

No. 34.

Welsh words by Rev: Owen Davies. (Eos Llechyd.)
English translation by Harold Boulton.

Old Welsh air arranged by
Arthur Somervell.

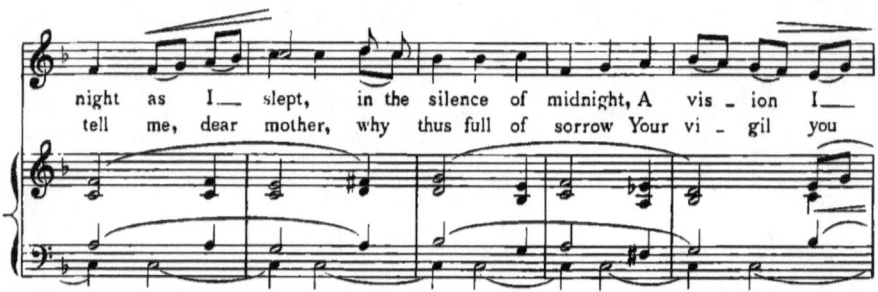

night as I slept, in the silence of midnight, A vis-ion I
tell me, dear mother, why thus full of sorrow Your vi-gil you

had. A wo-man's fair spi-rit rose soft-ly be-side me, In
keep. You fain would be with us, who loved you and lost you, And

(J. B. C. & Co. 10, 527.)

DREAM OF LITTLE RHYS.

Last night as I slept, in the silence of midnight
   A vision I had;
A woman's fair spirit rose softly beside me,
   In white was she clad.
She glided before me, she beckoned me kindly,
Where winds the Wye river my footsteps she drew,
And when she smiled sadly, my mother I knew.

"O tell me, dear mother, why thus full of sorrow
   Your vigil you keep?
You fain would be with us who loved you and lost you,
   And laid you to sleep.
Since you return never, your sweet soul I'll follow,
O, let me come to you!" Yet scarcely I spoke,
Ere alas! she had vanished; I trembled and woke.

Translated by HAROLD BOULTON.

BREUDDWYD RHYSYN BACH.

Rhyw noswaith mewn hûn
Breuddwydiais i freuddwyd, yn gweled rhyw fûn:
Mûn dyner ei serch
Yn cerdded yn araf ar lan afon Erch,
Edrychai yn bruddaidd
A gwelw a gwylaidd,
Gan rodio 'n arafaidd a thrymaidd ei cham,
Pan welais hi felly, mi gofiais fy Mam.

Ei gweled mewn hûn
Oedd imi'n llawenydd, O! ddedwydd o ddyn,
Ei threm oedd i mi
Er gwylaidd yr olwg, yn famaidd a chû,
Ond ciliodd o'r golau,
A chollais fy nagrau,
A hiraeth orlenwai fy mynwes ddinam,
Ond och! mi ddeffroais a chollais fy Mam.

EOS LLECHYD

The Ash Grove.

(HAROLD BOULTON.)

XXXV.

THE ASH GROVE.

The fair woodland bowers
Are peopled with flowers,
The trees, long forsaken,
   With green buds abound;
But trust not the weather
Though all bloom together;
When the ash trees awaken,
   Then summer's come round.

Ah! sweet was the pleasure,
In long days of leisure,
When life lay before us,
   In greenwood to rove;
Mild breezes were blowing,
Glad streamlets were flowing,
The birds sang in chorus
   Throughout the Ash Grove.

'Tis years since together
We hailed the warm weather,
When ash trees in maytime
   Awaken to life.
Old comrades, light-hearted,
Long since have departed,
Instead of youth's playtime,
   There's sorrow and strife.

Yet when woodland bowers
Are filled with fresh flowers,
'Neath trees of green splendour
   'Tis comfort to rove;
Though glimpses of gladness
Are mingled with sadness,
With memories most tender
   I seek the Ash Grove.

              HAROLD BOULTON.

LLWYN ON.

Mor swynol yw'r deildai
Y'n eigiol o flodau,
A'r coed yn hardd fintai
   Mewn blagur yn bod;
Ond coel 'does i'r tywydd
Llyd nes ceir yr arwydd;
Gwerdd onen rydd sicrwydd
   Fod hâf wedi dod.
Treuliasom yn hyfryd
Fyr ddyddiau ein hie'ngctyd,
Y'n agor 'r oedd bywyd
   O'n blaenau yn llon;
Awelon mwyn chwythent,
Y nentydd ymdreiglent,
Tra'r adar a byngcient
   Yn nghangau Llwyn On.

Pan olaf gydrodiem,
Yr hindda gyfarchem,
A'r onen feddyliem
   Oedd harddaf ei gwedd;
Cyfeillion twymgalon,
Pryd hyny'n gysurion—
Sy'n gorwedd yr awrhon
   Yn ddistaw mewn bedd.
Ond pan fydd y deildai
Y'n eigiol o flodau,
Diddanwch ddaw weithiau
   I lanw ein bron;
Yn gymysg a phrudd-der
Daw adgof fwyn dyner
Am oriau o bleser.
   Gaed gynt yn Llwyn On.

              G. M. PROBERT.

Myle Charaine.
(HAROLD BOULTON.)

XXXVI.

MYLE CHARAINE.*

O Myle Charaine, where got you your gold?
My heart it is heavy and lone,
A man that was murdered lies under the mould,
And the winds o'er the moorland moan.

Though Curragh with gold to heaven were piled,
My heart it is heavy and lone,
There's none would marry the murderer's child,
And the winds o'er the moorland moan.

Farewell to the father that did such a deed,
My heart it is heavy and lone,
A daughter's curse be the miser's meed,
And the winds o'er the moorland moan.

I'll lay me to sleep by the rising sea
My heart it is heavy and lone,
The wave my bridal sheet shall be,
And the winds o'er the moorland moan.

HAROLD BOULTON.

* The ten Manx verses here condensed represent a traditional dialogue between the first Manx man who provided his daughter with a dowry, and the girl herself, who upbraids him with the very questionable means employed to procure it, namely—the murder of some unoffending rich man. A literal translation of the Manx, by George Borrow, can be found in the Proceedings of the "Manx Society."

MYLE CHARAINE.

Question.—O Vylecharaine, craad hooar oo dty sthoyr?
My lomarcan daag oo mee;
Answer.—Nagh dooar mee'sy Churragh eh dowin, dowin dy liooar
As my lomarcan daag oo mee.

Question.—O Vylecharaine, craad hooar oo dty sthock?
My lomarcan daag oo me;
Answer.—Nagh dooar mee'sy Churragh eh eddyr daa vlock,
As my lomarcan daag oo mee.

Question.—O Vylecharaine, craad hooar oo ny tayd?
My lomarcan daag oo mee;
Answer.—Nagh dooar mee'sy Churragh eh eddyr daa 'aid.
As my lomarcan daag oo mee.

Hug mee my eggey-varree as my eggey-lieen,
My lomarcan daag oo mee;
As hug mee dow-ollee son to ghyr dán' neon,
As my lomarcan daag oo mee.

Daughter.—O Yishig, O Yishig, ta mee nish goaill nearey.
My lomarcan daag oo mee;
Tóu goll gys y cheoill ayns dy charraneyn varey.
As my lomarcan daag oo mee.

Daughter.—O Yishig, O Yishig, jeeagh er my vraaghyn stoamey
My lomarcan daag oo mee;
As uss goll my geayrt ayns dty charraneyn vaney,
As dy lomarcan daag oo mee.

She un charrane ghoo, as fer elley vane,
My lomarcan daag oo mee;
Vórts Vylecharaine goll dy ghoolish jesarn,
As my lomarcan daag oo mee.

Daughter.—Shee daa phiyr oashyr, as un phiyr vraag,
My lomarcan daag oo mee;
Cheau uss Vylecharaine aynskiare-bluantyn-jeig,
As my lomarcan daag oo mee.

Father.—O vuddee, O vuddee, chalhiass dhyts goaill nearey
My lomarcan daag oo mee;
Son táyms ayns my chishtey ver orts dy ghearey
As my lomarcan daag oo mee.

Execration.—My hiaght mynney-mollaght ort, O Vylecharaine,
My lomarcan daag oo mee;
Son uss ván chied ghooinney hug toghyr da mraane
As my lomarcan daag oo mee.

TRADITIONAL.

When in Death.

(THOMAS MOORE.)

XXXVII.

WHEN IN DEATH.

№ 37.

English words by Thomas Moore.
Irish translation by Archbishop Mac Hale.

Old Irish Air.
Arranged by Arthur Somervell.

WHEN IN DEATH.

When in death I shall calm recline,
  Oh bear my heart to my mistress dear;
Tell her it liv'd upon smiles and wine
  Of the brightest hue, while it linger'd here.
Bid her not shed one tear of sorrow,
  To sully a heart so brilliant and light;
But balmy drops of the red grape borrow,
  To bathe the relic from morn till night.

When the light of my song is o'er,
  Then take my harp to your ancient hall;
Hang it up at that friendly door
  Where weary travellers love to call:
Then if some Bard, who roams forsaken,
  Revive its soft note in passing along.
Oh! let one thought of its master waken
  Your warmest smile for the child of song!

Keep this cup, that is now o'erflowing,
  To grace your revel when I'm at rest;
Never, oh, never, its balm bestowing
  On lips that beauty hath seldom blest!
But when some warm devoted lover
  To her he adores shall bathe its brim,
Then, then my spirit around shall hover,
  And hallow each drop that foams for him.

THOMAS MOORE.

TRÁ CIÚIN N-DÉIS BHAIS.

Trá ciuin n-déis bháis bheidheas sínte claon,
  Béir cum mo chéile ghradhaighe mo chroidhe;
Dí innis gur chothuigh é smig' a's sgaith síon.
Co'ad as air an t-saoghal so, 'nna comhnuidhe bhí,
Léi, abair gan silt aon deor amháin gola
  A líonfadh le lionndubh brón a croidhe;
Acht bmon a thairgeadh de chaor síon fola,
  Chum an fuighioll a bheith falctha gach lá a's oidhche.

Nuair bheidheas so!us mo cheol' 'nna luidhe,
  Beir mo chlairseach go d-tí do lann;
Croch í suas le h-ais dorus an tighe
  'Bh-faghann siubhalaidh tuirseach sgith failteamhail ann.
'S tra deanfas bard bocht seachrain' seasadh',
  A dusacht a teuda as suan go rinn,
Bidheadh cuimhne air an bh-file air leis í, a lasad,
  Do sinig do leanbh na g-ceolta' binn.

Conbhuig, n's e 'nois faoi mhaol, an sgala,
  Chum n-eis mo 'mtheacht, bheith air do chlar,
Acht béul gan cuman aig fleidh no dala
  Go deo ní bhlaisfidh deor as a bharr.
Acht ma bhidheann fear fíor gan claon í mhealladh,
  A's olfas d'a run nach dual a chradh,
Mo ghaethe beidh 'g eitioll teacht ann reir ghealladh
  'Gus beannugadh gach bmon de'n g-cuach 'sa tra.

ARCHBISHOP MAC HALE.

The Gentle Maiden.
(HAROLD BOULTON.)

XXXVIII.

THE GENTLE MAIDEN.

Nº 38.

English words by HAROLD BOULTON.
Irish translation by Dʀ Douglas Hyde.

Old Irish Air.
Arranged by Arthur Somervell.

Andante.

PIANO. *p*

There's one that is pure as an an — gel, And fair as the flow'rs of May, ——— They call her the gen — tle mai — den Where-ever she takes her way. ———

Though part — ed a — far from my dar — ling, I dream of her ev'ry-where, ——— The sound of her voice is a — bout — me, The spell of her pres — ence there. ——— Her eyes have the glance of And whe — ther my prayers be

(J.B.C & Cº 10,527.)

THE GENTLE MAIDEN.

There's one that is pure as an angel,
  And fair as the flowers of May,
They call her the gentle maiden
  Wherever she takes her way.
Her eyes have the glance of sunlight,
  As it brightens the blue sea wave,
And more than the deep sea treasure,
  The love of her heart I crave.

Though parted afar from my darling,
  I dream of her everywhere,
The sound of her voice is about me,
  The spell of her presence there.
And whether my prayers be granted,
  Or whether she pass me by,
The face of that gentle maiden
  Will follow me till I die.

HAROLD BOULTON.

AN MHAIGHDEAN CHAOIN.

Tá maighdean ann, díleas mar aingeall,
  Chomh sáimh leis an mBealtaine Buidhe;
Air a d-tugaid "caoimh-inghean" mar ainm,
  Is múinte 's is maiseamhail í.
Tá a súile mar taithneamh na gréine
  Ag lasadh le sgéimh ar an tonn,
Agus b-feárr liom a grádh agam féin
  'Ná an móad tá i d-Tír na long.
Cidh sgartha óm' stóirin atá mó,
  Dar liom-sa 's im' láthair í,
Im' chluais a guth luthgháireach,
  Agus a draoidheacht a gáire i m' chroidhe.
Má 's diúltadh cruaidh tá 'n dán dam,
  No truagh, no cia bó nidh,
Ní sgarfaidh a searc go bráth liom .
  'S ní chlaoidhfidh an Bás féin í.

Dr. DOUGLAS HYDE.

Kitty Magee.

(F. A. FAHY.)

XXXIX.

KITTY MAGEE.

I've kissed and courted them all,
Gentle and simple, short, and medium, and tall;
But kept a merry heart free,
Till it was stole unknownst by Kitty Magee.
Her laughing face, her slender waist,
Her lips might tempt a saint to taste;
Oh, sure it was small blame to me,
To lose my heart to Kitty Magee.

'Twas down at Ballina fair,
Cailins and boys were gaily tripping it there,
And I the soul of the spree,
When I set eyes on charming Kitty Magee.
Her smile so sweet, her step so neat,
Hide and seek her two little feet;
Gliding just like a swan at sea,
Handsome, winsome Kitty Magee.

And now I'm dreaming all day,
Sighing from dark to dawn, and wasting away,
Like a lone bird on a tree,
Pining the long hours through for Kitty Magee.
At dance or wake, no sport I make;
Home or out no pleasure I take,
Nothing at all I hear or see,
But makes me think of Kitty Magee.

Oh, how will I any one face,
Kitty *asthore*, if you don't pity my case?
'Tis tired of living I'll be
If I don't win my darling Kitty Magee.
Oh whisper, dear, the Shrove is near:
Say the word I'm dying to hear.
Promise me soon my own you'll be,
Roguish, coaxing Kitty Magee.

F. A. FAHY.

Shule Agra.

(A. P. GRAVES.)

XL.

* The Sumptuary law of the times apparently required the beggar-woman to wear a red petticoat.

SHULE AGRA!

His hair was black, his eye was blue,
His arm was stout, his word was true;
I wish in my heart I was with you.
    *Go-thee-thu, mavourneen slaun!
Shule, shule, shule agra!
Only death can ease my woe,
Since the lad of my heart from me did go,
    Go-thee-thu, mavourneen slaun!

'Tis oft I sat on my true love's knee,
Many a fond story he told to me,
He told me things that ne'er shall be,
    Go-thee-thu, mavourneen slaun.
Shule, shule, shule agra! †
Only death can ease my woe,
Since the lad of my heart from me did go,
    Go-thee-thu, mavourneen slaun!

I sold my rock, ‡ I sold my reel;
When my flax was spun, I sold my wheel,
To buy my love a sword of steel,
    Go-thee-thu, mavourneen slaun!
Shule, shule, shule agra!
Only death can ease my woe,
Since the lad of my heart from me did go,
    Go-thee-thu, mavourneen slaun!

But when King James was forced to flee,
The § Wild Geese spread their wings to sea,
And bore mabouchal ‖ far from me,
    Go-thee-thu, mavourneen slaun!
Shule, shule, shule agra!
Only death can ease my woe,
Since the lad of my heart from me did go,
    Go-thee-thu, mavourneen slaun!

I saw them sail from Brandon Hill,
Then down I sat and cried my fill,
That every tear would turn a mill,
    Go-thee-thu, mavourneen slaun.
Shule, shule, shule agra!
Only death can ease my woe,
Since the lad of my heart from me did go,
    Go-thee-thu, mavourneen slaun!

I wish the King would return to reign,
And bring my true love back again;
I wish, and wish, but I wish in vain,
    Go-thee-thu, mavourneen slaun.
Shule, shule, shule agra!
Only death can ease my woe,
Since the lad of my heart from me did go,
    Go-thee-thu, mavourneen slaun!

I'll dye my petticoat, ¶ I'll dye it red,
And round the world I'll beg my bread,
Till I find my love alive or dead,
    Go-thee-thu, mavourneen slaun.
Shule, shule, shule agra!
Only death can ease my woe,
Since the lad of my heart from me did go,
    Go-thee-thu, mavourneen slaun!

ALFRED PERCEVAL GRAVES.

*Farewell, my darling!   †Come, come, my love!   ‡Rock and reel—two parts of the Irish spinning wheel.
§The Irish Jacobites who left their country for service in the French army, when the cause of James II. was lost.
‖Mabouchal—My boy.   ¶The sumptuary law of the times apparently required beggar women to wear red petticoats.

SIUBHAIL A GHRAIDH,
(SHUILE AGRA.)

A bhuachaillín aoibhinn aluinn oíg
Budh leathan do chroidhe, budh deas do phog
Mo leun gan mise leat tein go deo
    'So go dteidh tu a mhuirnín slan.

    Siubhail, siubhail, siubhail a ghraidh,
    Ní'l leigheas le faghail acht leigheas an Bhais,
    O d'fhag tu mise is bocht mo chas
        'S go dteidh tu a mhuirnín slan.

Is minic do bhreug se me air a ghluin,
Ag cur a sgeil dam féin i n-aimhail,
Acht cbaill me e, agus e mo run
    'S go dteidh tu a mhuirnín slan.

Snáomh me lion a's dhiol me e
Dhiol me dho mo thuirna féin
Cheannuigh me cloidheamh do ghradh mo chleibh
    'S go dteidh tu a mhuirnín slan.

Acht cuireadh ar Righ Seumas ruaig,
A's d'imthigh na Geana leis ar luathas,
A's d'imthigh mo bhuachaill leo, mo nuair,
    'S go dteidh tu a mhuirnín slan.

Do shuidh me sios ar thulach mor
Ag deareadh air a huing faoi seol,
Thionntochainn muileann le gach deor
    'S go dteidh tu a mhuirnín slan.

Mo leun gan Seumas teacht i g-croin
Is e do sgaptadh uaim mo bhron
Acht ní'l aon mhaith I ngol, ochon,
    'S go dteidh tu a mhuirnín slan.

Do dheargfainn féin mo ghuna ban,
As chuairteochainn an domhan iomlan
Go bhfagh me marbh e, no slan.
    'S go dteidh tu a mhuirnín slan.

    Siubhal, siubhal, siubhal a ghraidh
    N'íl leigheas le faghail acht leigheas an Bhais,
    O d'fhag tu mise is bocht mo chas
        'S go dteidh tu a mhuirnín slan.

DR. DOUGLAS HYDE.

The Castle of Dromore.

(HAROLD BOULTON.)

XLI.

THE CASTLE OF DROMORE.

№ 41. (IRISH LULLABY.)

English words by Harold Boulton.
Irish translation by Dr Douglas Hyde.

Old Irish Air.
Arranged by Arthur Somervell.

October winds lament around the Castle of Dromore, — But peace is in her lofty halls, *Mo páiste veg ashtore; My dearest treasure store; Though autumn leaves may

* Literally, "Little child, my treasure."

(J.B.C & Co 10,327.)

THE CASTLE OF DROMORE.
(IRISH LULLABY.)

October winds lament around the Castle of Dromore,
But peace is in her lofty halls, mo páiste veg asthore;
Though autumn leaves may droop and die, a bud of spring are you—
Sing hushaby lullaloo lo lan, sing hushaby lullaloo.

Bring no ill-will to hinder us—my helpless babe and me,
Dread spirits of the Blackwater, Clan Eoghan's wild banshee;
For Holy Mary, pitying us, in heaven for grace doth sue—
Sing hushaby lullaloo lo lan, sing hushaby lullaloo.

Take time to thrive, my rose of hope, in the garden of Dromore;
Take heed, young eaglet, till your wings have feathers fit to soar.
A little rest, and then the world is full of work to do—
Sing hushaby lullaloo lo lan, sing hushaby lullaloo.

HAROLD BOULTON.

* Literally, "Little child, my treasure."

CAISLEÁN AN DROMA-MHÓIR.

Tá gaotha an gheimhridh sgallta fuar, thart thimchioll an Drom'-mhóir,
Acht ann sna alla ta siothchán, mo phaisde beag astor,
Ta gach sean-duilleog dul air crith, acht is óg an beannglan thu,
Seinnfimid lóithín ló ló lán, lóithín a's lul la lú.

Nár thig aon droch-rud idir mé's mo naoidheanán gan bhrón,
Nar thig aon tais ó'n Abhainn Mhóir na Bean-sidhe Chloinne Eoghain,
Tá Muire Máthair ós ár g-cionn ag iarradh grása dúinn;
Seinnfimid lóithín ló ló lán, lóithín a's lul la lú.

A Róis mo chroidhe, a Slaithín ur a's gharrdha an Drom'-mhóir,
Bí ag fás go mbeidh gach cleite beag mar sgiathán iolair mhóir,
Agus léim ann sin air fad an t-saoghail, oibrigh a's saothraigh clú;
Seinnfimid lóithín ló ló lán, lóithín a's lul la lú.

Dr. DOUGLAS HYDE.

The Snowy-Breasted Pearl.
(DR. PETRIE.)

XLII.

THE SNOWY BREASTED PEARL.

There's a colleen fair as May,
For a year and for a day
I have sought by every way, her heart to gain;
There's no art of tongue or eye,
Fond youths with maidens try,
But I've tried with ceaseless sigh—Yet tried in vain.
If to France or far off Spain,
She'd cross the wat'ry main,
To see her face again,—The seas I'd brave.
And if 'tis heaven's decree,
That mine she may not be,
May the Son of Mary, me—In mercy save.

Oh, thou blooming milk-white dove,
To whom I've given true love,
Do not even thus reprove—My constancy.
There are maidens would be mine,
With wealth in hand and kine,
If my heart would but incline—To turn from thee.
But a kiss with welcome bland,
And touch of thy fair hand,
Are all that I'd demand,—Wouldst thou not spurn;
For if not mine, dear girl,
Oh! snowy-breasted Pearl!
May I never from the Fair—With life return!

Dr. PETRIE.

PEARLA AN BHROLLAIGH BHÁIN.

Atá cailín deas am chrádh,
Le bliadhain agus le lá,
Is ní fhéadhaim a fágháil le bréagadh
Ní'l aisde chlis le radh,
Dá g-canaid fir le mná.
Nár chaitheamair gan tábhacht léi-si:
Do'n Frainc nó do'n Spain,
Dá d-téigheadh mo ghradh,
Go raghainn-sí gach lá dá féachain,
Is mar an bh-fuil sé a n-dán,
Duinn an ainnfhir chiuin soo d'fhágháil,
Uch! Mac Muire na n-grás d'ár saoradh.

'Sa chailín chailce bhláth,
Dá d-tugas searc is grádh,
Ná tabhair-sí gach tráth dham éradh;
'Sa liacht ainnfhir mhín am dheáigh
Re buaibh is maoin 'na láimh,
Da n-gabhamais a d'áit cóile:
Póg is míle fáilte,
'S barraidhe geal do lámh,
Ase 'n-iarrfuinn-sí go bráth mar spreidh leat:
'S mar an damhsa ta tu a n-dán,
A Phéarla an Bhrollaigh bháin,
Nár thig mise slan ó'n n-aonac.

TRADITIONAL.

The Wild Hills of Clare.

(F. A. FAHY.)

XLIII.

THE WILD HILLS OF CLARE.

N°: 43.

Words by F. A. Fahy.

Old Irish Air.
Arranged by Arthur Somervell.

THE WILD HILLS OF CLARE.

Through lone years of exile I sighed to be home,
Once more with the friends of my boyhood to roam,
And to ask the first love of my bosom to share
A home in the heart of the Wild Hills of Clare.

From lone years of exile I came back once more,
To find that my false love a rival's name bore,
And the friends of my boyhood I sought everywhere,
But none knew me now mid the Wild Hills of Clare.

Oh Wild Hills, alone mid my fond hopes o'erthrow,
You still wear the smile that you wore long ago,
Oh I'll welcome with gladness the end of life's care,
A grave in the heart of the Wild Hills of Clare.

F. A. FAHY.

GHARBH-CHNOIC CHLÁIR.

Le bliadhantaibh geura, 's mé 'm' dhíbearteach truaigh,
Do smuain mé ar Éirinn, ár oileán na mbuaidh,
Ag súil le Mac Dé go mbeidh' áras le fághail
Le céud-shearc mo chleibh ameasg garbh-chnoc Chláir.

Ar d-teacht dam a-bhaile a's tíorthaibh í g-céin,
Och, fuaireas go ndearna sí feall orm féin,
Ní raibh aithne ag daoinibh ar m'eudan, mo chrádh,
Is mo choimhightheach bhí me 'measg garbh-chnoc Chláir.

Athruighthear gach nidh liom, acht sibh-se amáin,
Tá sibh-se mar bhi sibh, a ghaibh-cnuic Chlair
Chomh lom-bheannach, árd-pheucach, soillseach, a's breágh,
Go raibh m'uaigh í n-dán dam measg garbh chnoc Chláir.

Dr. DOUGLAS HYDE

Little Mary Cassidy
(F. A. FAHY.)

XLIV.

rai - son that I am not now the boy I used to be; Oh, she
heard her sing an Ir - ish song till tears came in my eyes; And
kind - ness of her kis - ses, or the glancing of her eye? Oh, though

bates the beau - ties all that we read a - bout in his - to - ry, Sure
ev - er since that blessed hour I'm dreaming day and night of her; The
trou - bles throng my breast, sure they'd soon go to the right a - bout, If I

half the coun - try side's as lost for her as me. Trav - el
divil a wink of sleep I get from bed to rise. Her
thought the cur - ly head would nes - tle there, by'n, bye. Take

(J. B. C. & Co 10 527.)

LITTLE MARY CASSIDY.

Oh, 'tis little Mary Cassidy's the cause of all my misery,
    The raison that I am not now the boy I used to be;
Oh, she bates the beauties all that we read about in history,
    Sure half the country-side's as lost for her as me.

Travel Ireland up and down—hill, village, vale and town—
    Girl like my " cailin donn "* you'll be looking for in vain;
Oh, I'd rather live in poverty with little Mary Cassidy
    Than Emperor, without her be, o'er Germany or Spain.

'Twas at the dance at Darmody's that first I caught a sight of her,
    And heard her sing an Irish song, till tears came in my eyes;
And ever since that blessed hour I'm dreaming day and night of her;
    The divil a wink of sleep I get from bed to rise.

Her cheek the rose in June, her song the lark in tune,
    Working, resting, night or noon, she never laves my mind;
Oh, till singing by my cabin fire sits little Mary Cassidy,
    'Tis little aise or happiness I'm sure I'll ever find.

What is wealth, or what is fame, or what is all that people fight about
    To the kindness of her kisses or the glancing of her eye?
Oh, though troubles throng my breast, sure they'd soon go to the right-about,
    If I thought the curly hair would nestle there, by'n'bye.

Take all I own to-day—kith, kin, and care away,
    Ship them all across the say, or to the frozen zone,
Lave me here an orphan bare—*but O lave me Mary Cassidy*,
    I never would feel lonesome with the two of us alone.

F. A. FAHY.

* Pronounced "colleen dhown"—Angl. "brown-haired girl."

The Gaol of Clonmel.

(F. A. FAHY.)

XLV.

THE GAOL OF CLONMEL.

№ 45.

English words by F. A. Fahy.
Irish translation by Dr Douglas Hyde.

Old Irish Air
Arranged by Arthur Somervell

THE GAOL OF CLONMEL.

While the bright flow'rs are blowing,
While the glad spring is glowing,
My young life sworn away, in Clonmel gaol I lie;
From my bride broken-hearted,
From my friends harshly parted,
For a crime not my own, doomed at daybreak to die.

Oh, my love, never more shall your fond arms embrace me,
By cold chains they're replaced, in the gaol of Clonmalla.

If one name I had spoken,
Had I made sign or token,
In the pure air of freedom I'd breathe once again.
But my life wrecked and blighted,
By no wrong shall be righted,
Nor my name linked with shame in the hearts of true men.

When the friends that I loved, I leave weeping behind me,
They shall not blush to speak of the gaol of Clonmalla.

Farewell, wife of my bosom,
'Farewell, youth's fairest blossom!
Oh, 'tis hard thus to part with all life held most dear.
But my soul Heav'n sustaining,
All its wild grief restraining,
On the grim face of Fate I can gaze without fear.

No! Though Death wait without, he no craven shall find me,
When at dawn I'm led forth from the gaol of Clonmalla.

F. A. FAHY.

PRIÓSÚN CHLUAIN-MEALA.

Tá taithneamh na gréin' ann,
'S an fhuiseog 'sna spéarthaibh,
Acht i b-priosún am' aonar i gCluain-meala táim,
Ó mhnaoi óig mo chroidhe-se,
'S óm' cháirdibh táim sgaoilthe,
Air son coir nach ndearnas tá an bás dam i ndán.

A mhúirnín mo chroidhe-se m'fheicfead thu coidhche,
Faoi shlabhrachaibh iarainn i gCluain-meala táim.

Ní'l a acht rud beag le rádh—
Rud nach ndéarfad go bráth—
Ag braith air mo cháirdibh, s do thiucfainn-se slán;
Acht ní fheudthaion bheith beo,
Air an maragadh so,
A's ní caillfidh me m'onóir, 's an bás dam i ndan.

Dar mo láimh ní béidh náire go bráth air mo cháirdibh,
Nuair déarfaid, "I gCluain-meala fuair sé a bhás."

A bhean dhíleas mo chróidhe,
Cuirim slán leat a choidhch',
Cuirim cúl leis an t-saoghal, agus 'leat-sa go bráth,
Acht ní chaoinfead "ochón"
A's ní fheicfear mo bhrón,
Nuair thiucfas amárach lucht-crochta dom' chradh.

Ní thiucfaidh aon sganuradh ná faitchios air m'anam,
Acht mar ghaisgidheach rachfad i g-coinne mo bháis.

DR. DOUGLAS HYDE.

Drimin Dhu.

(F. A. FAHY.)

XLVI.

DRIMIN DHU.

Nº 46.

English words by F. A. FAHY.
Irish translation by Dr. Douglas Hyde.

Old Irish Air.
Arranged by ARTHUR SOMERVELL.

She's_ gone, oh! Drim-in Dhu, that_
Who_ now, my Drim-in Dhu, our_

loved you dear, No_ more at
joy will be, The world is

*Pronounced "Oh Drimin dhoo dhee-lish mav-rone gudh yo!"
Oh dear Black Cow, my grief for ever. (J. B. C. & Co. 10 527.)

DRIMIN DHU.

She's gone, oh Drimin Dhu, that loved you dear,
No more at milking time her song you'll hear
Your kind, fond mistress now lies cold and low,
Oh, Drimin Dhu deelish, mo bhron go deo.*

Oh, fair her young face looked that day of pride,
When with you, her portion small, I called her bride ;
No king I envied then on earth below—
Oh, Drimin Dhu deelish, mo bhron go deo.

Who now, my Drimin Dhu, our joy will be?
The world is desolate, for you and me ;
Life's lost for evermore its summer glow,
Oh, Drimin Dhu deelish, mo bhron go deo.

Oh, voice of gentleness ! oh, looks of light !
Oh, heart of tenderness, noon, morn and night !
Soon, soon, in search of you, from earth I'll go,
Oh, Drimin Dhu deelish, mo bhron go deo.

F. A. FAHY.

* Pronounced "Oh, Drimmin dhoo dhee-lish mav-rone gudh-yo"—
"Oh, dear black cow, my grief for ever."

DRUIMFHIONN DUBH.
(DRIMIN DHU.)

An té sin do bhligh tu, a Druimfhionn Dubh O,
Cá bhfuil sí, ca bhfuil sí, óir ní'l sí ann so ?
Ní fheicfimid, chualaidh mé, í níos mó,
Mo Dhruimfhionn Dubh díleas, mo bhrón go deo !

Mo chailín geal áluinn ! nár fheuch sí go sáimh,
An lá sin do chuir mé an fáinne air a láimh !
Ní mhaoidhinn air Righ Seorsa a cheud míle bo,
Da mbeidh' sise as tu liom a Dhruimfhionn Dubh O !

Nach fuar é an saoghal, a Dhruimfhionn Dubh O ?
Gan suaimhneas anois ann, gan seun a's gan sogh ;
Ní'l i g-ceileabhar na n-eun act mar ob-ob-o,
O d'imthigh si uainne, mo bhrón go deo.

Budh bhinn liom a laoi a's a béilín beag óg,
Budh liom-sa a croidhe, a's budh liom-sa a póg,
Ní fhánfad gan í air an droch-shaoghal so,
'S a Dhruimfhionn Dubh díleas, mo bhrón go deo.

Dr. DOUGLAS HYDE.

Barney Brallaghan.
(A. P. GRAVES.)

XLVII.

BARNEY BRALLAGHAN.

On a night of June,
   A fine young Irish farmer
Thus takes up his tune,
   Complaining to his charmer;
" 'Tis a twelve-month, Kate,
   Since I first came courtin,
Yet my suit you trate
   Still with cruel sportin'.

    Och, just say
      You'll be Mrs. Brallaghan!
    Don't say nay,
      Charming Kitty Callaghan!

Eyes whose heavenly ray
   Shot through shadowy fringes;
Cost me in one day,
   Twenty thousand twinges.
Dimpled chin and cheek,
   Whose hue just sets me silly,
Since 'tis hide and seek
   Betwixt the rose and lily.

    Beauty's star,
      Charming Kitty Callaghan,
    That's what you are,
      Sighs poor Barney Brallaghan.

And though there's just a doubt,
   If I've enough of cash, dear;
You've the lovely mout',
   And I the grand moustache, dear.
You've the genteel taste,
   And I'm the boy to hit it;
You've the perfect waist,
   And I the arm to fit it.

    So just say
      You'll be Mrs. Brallaghan;
    Don't say nay,
      Charming Kitty Callaghan!"

A. P. GRAVES.

The Tree in the Wood.

(HAROLD BOULTON.)

XLVIII.

THE TREE IN THE WOOD.
(OR YOUNG DENIS)

N⁰ 48.

English words by HAROLD BOULTON.
Irish translation by D? DOUGLAS HYDE.

Old Irish Air
Arranged by ARTHUR SOMERVELL.

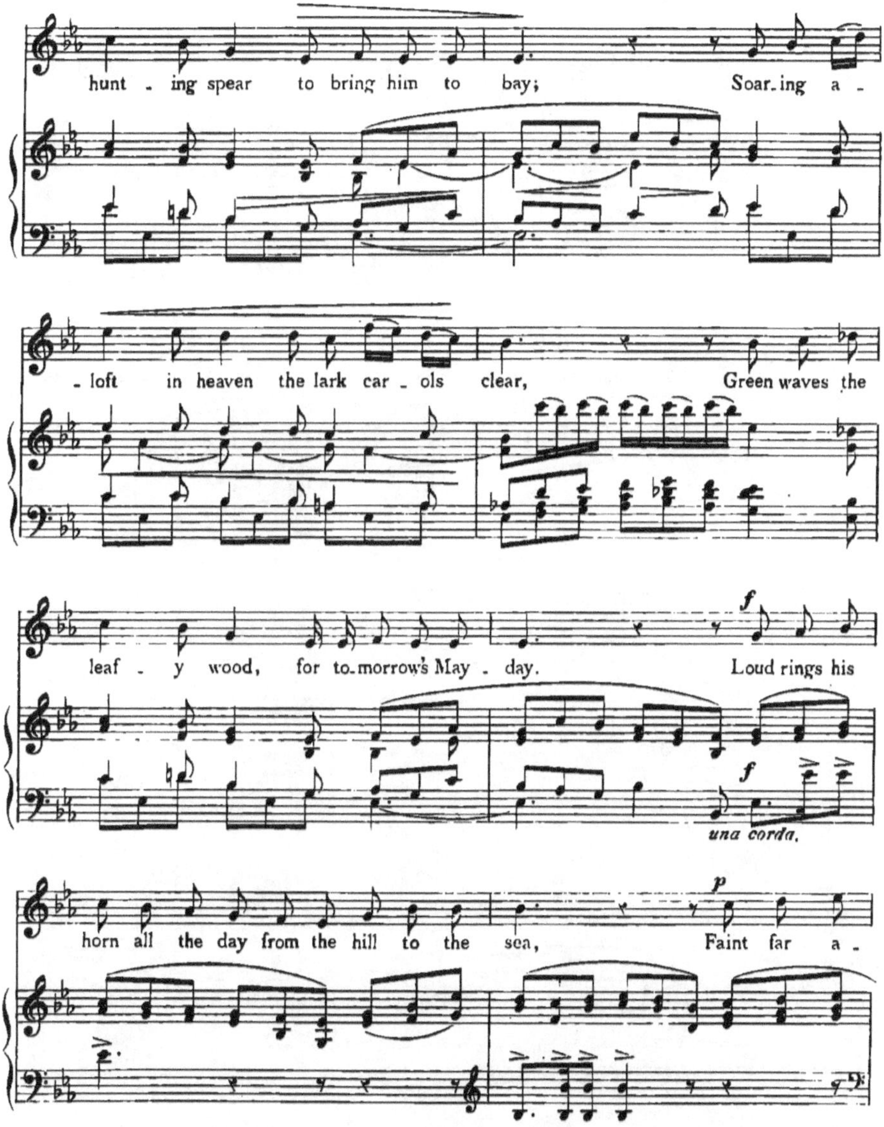
hunt - ing spear to bring him to bay; Soar-ing a -
- loft in heaven the lark car - ols clear, Green waves the
leaf - y wood, for to-morrow's May - day. Loud rings his
f
f
una corda.
horn all the day from the hill to the sea, Faint far a -
p

THE TREE IN THE WOOD.

Or YOUNG DENIS.

Over the hill young Denis follows the deer,
   Hound, horn, and hunting spear to bring him to bay;
Soaring aloft in heaven the lark carols clear,
   Green waves the leafy wood, for to-morrow's Mayday.
Loud rings his horn all the day from the hill to the sea,
   Faint far away through the wood till the fall of the night ;
Weary he rests with his hounds 'neath the hollow oak tree,
   Foolish he sinks into sleep by the silver moonlight.

Fairer than mortal rose a maid from the brier,
   Singing a song more sweet than mortal can tell,
Touched him on brow and lip with kisses of fire,
   Gave him to drink the wine of magical spell.
Swift to the dance of the fairies she bore him away,
   Crowned him her lover, and king of the mad revelry ;
Dead lay his hounds on the sward at the dawn of Mayday,
   Gone was young Denis that slept 'neath the hollow oak tree.

Over the hill a horn the forester hears,
   When leaves are waving green and to-morrow's Mayday;
Leading the dance at night a maiden appears,
   Linked with a huntsman clad in gallant array.
Masterless now are his cattle that low on the hill,
   Sad his companions that wonder and wait him in vain,
Bowed in the ashes his mother, that mourns for him still,
   Back to the sunlight young Denis comes never again.

HAROLD BOULTON.

DINIS ÓG AG FIADHACH.

Chuaidh Dinis amach air na sléibhtibh air lorg na bhfiadh,
   Le n-a choin a's a stoc a's a sgian 's a shleigh ann a láimh
'S budh bhinn leis 'sna neulltaibh shuas an fhuiseoigín liath,
   Air maidin lae Bealtaine 'g gabháil a h-abhráin go sáimh
Do mhúsgail sé fuaim na macalla go meadhrach 's na binn,
   O chrann agus carraig, ó shliabh ó chnoc agus gleann,
Ne gur chodluigh an laoch, 's é tuirseach de'n fhiadhach, ann sin,
   Faoi sholus na gealaigh' leis féin, 's ó faoi sgáile na g-crann.

D' eirigh ó sgeich le n-a thaoibh-sean an réultan mná.
   Budh bhinne an ceol ann a beul 'na caoin-chláirseach na sidh.
Do phóg sí a mhala go minic le pógaibh grádh,
   Agus leag sí a draigheacht go trom air a chliabh 's a chroidhe.
Ag ringce na sidh-bhean do rug sí an laoch, le mian,
   'S chuir fáinne de 'n ór air a mheur agus cró:n air a cheann,
Bhí a choin uile marbh air maidin trá d'eirigh an ghrian,
   A's Dinis óg imthighthe a's radarc, faoi sgáile na g-crann.

Gach Bealtaine séidthear an stoc sin, stoc Dinis, 's an ngleann,
   Agus cluintear an fhuaim ann san gcoill sin Lá Bealtaine Buidhe
Agus cidhtear óg-mhaighdean ag ringce faoi dhuileabhar na g-crann
   'S fear-seilge léithe, 's is iongantach áluinn í.
Tá anois a chuid eallaigh gan aodhaire leo féin air an gcnoc,
   Is brónach 'una dhiaigh anois a lucht cumainn a's graidh,
Tá a mhathair 'g fás liath le súil do bhreith 'g eisteacht a stoic,—
   Acht uí fheicfidhear Dinis 'san t-saoaghal so choidhche go bráth.

DR. DOUGLAS HYDE.

Kathleen ni Hoolhaun.

(F. A. FAHY.)

XLIX.

KATHLEEN NI HOOLHAUN.*

Original Irish Words by WILLIAM HEFFERNAN.
English words by F. A. FAHY.

Old Irish Air
Arranged by ARTHUR SOMERVELL.

* One of the allegorical names by which Ireland was known in Irish song.

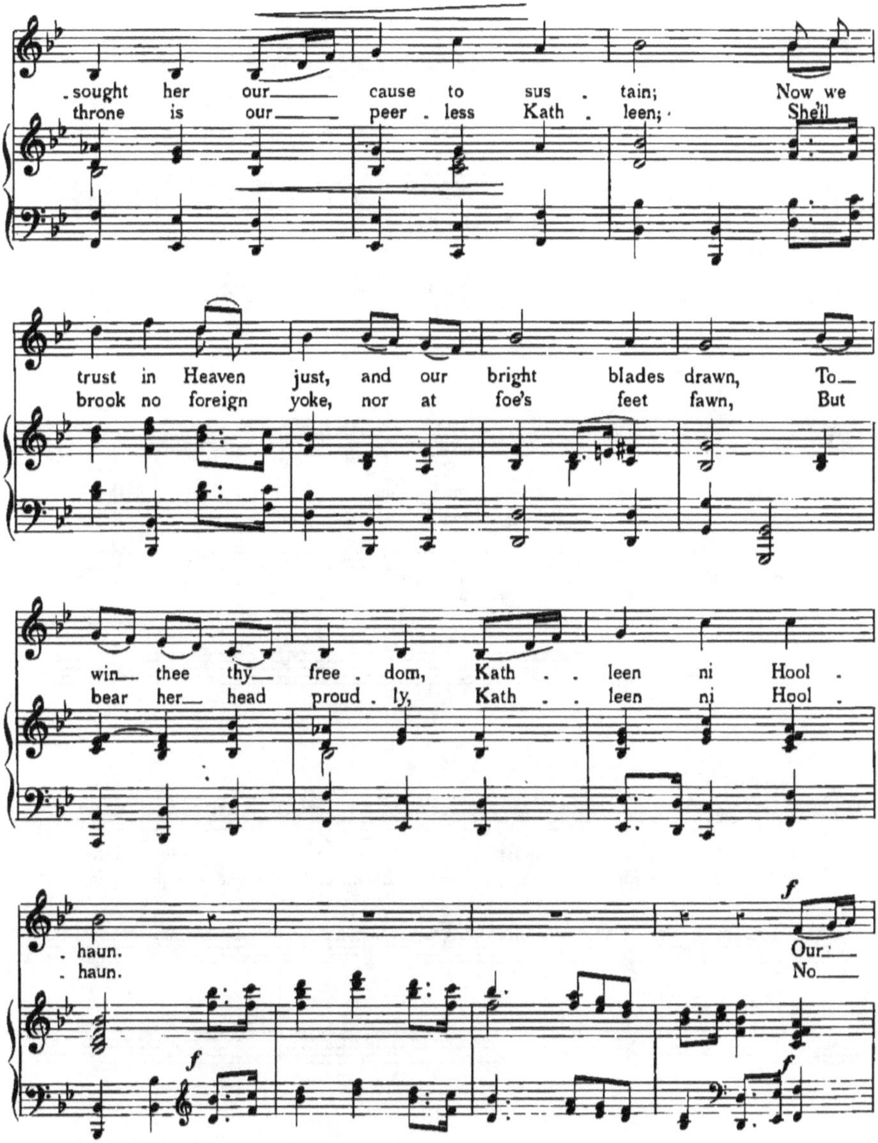
-sought her our cause to sus - tain; Now we
throne is our peer - less Kath - leen; She'll
trust in Heaven just, and our bright blades drawn, To
brook no foreign yoke, nor at foe's feet fawn, But
win thee thy free - dom, Kath - - leen ni Hool -
bear her head proud - ly, Kath - - leen ni Hool -
-haun. Our
-haun. No
f
f
f

KATHLEEN NI HOOL'HAUN.*

(A Jacobite Song.—From the original Irish).

Too long o'er the water we looked to Spain,
And vainly besought her our cause to sustain;
Now we trust in Heaven just and our bright blades drawn,
To win thee thy freedom, Kathleen ni Hool'haun.

Our priests all are chanting, our fond ones weep,
Our bards loud exulting the wild harp strings sweep,
While we wait with hearts elate, on each field and bawn,
Thy Prince's home-coming, Kathleen ni Hool'haun.

No withered grim crone is our hearts' loved Queen;
Fit mate for a throne is our peerless Kathleen:
She'll brook no foreign yoke, nor at foe's feet fawn,
But bear her head proudly, Kathleen ni Hool'haun.

No more shall she languish in bondage drear,
Her long night of anguish its end draweth near;
Each height leaps into light—'tis the looked-for dawn!
Dost hear thy Prince call thee, Kathleen ni Hool'haun?

F. A. FAHY.

* Kathleen Ní Hoolahaun was one of the allegorical names by which Ireland was known in Irish song ("Ní" = modern "O").

CAITILIN NÍ UALLACHAIN.

Measamoid, nach calm rín, do'n bhuairt san Spainn,
Acht mealla slighe, chum catha cloidhimh, do thabhairt a d-tráith
Beidh Galla arísh, da leagadh siós le lúth ár lámhaibh,
Agus mac an Rígh, ag Caitilín Ní Uallacháin!

Tá ár g-cléire, a g-caomh-ghuith, a súil le Críost,
'S ár n-eigsi go réimeach, 's a g cúmha dul díobh:
Gaodhail bhocht Innis Eilge go súgach, síodhach,
Roimh Sheamhus mhic Sheamuis, 's an Diuic tar toinn.

Ná measadaois gur caile chíor ár stuaire stáid,
Na caillichín, 'na g-crapadois a g-cuaill-bheag cnamha;
Cia fadha luighe dhi le fearaibh coimhtheach gan suaimhneas d'fhagal
Atá suith an Righ a g-Caitilín Ní Uallachain!

Is iada sinn ag faire aris, le fuasgail d'fhághail,
Nár stalaraidhe, gan balcaisidhe, 'na luadh 'nár láimh;
Beidh barca líonta air bárra taoide, 's fuaim air sáil,
Le mac an Righ, chum Caitilín Ní Uallacháin!

WILLIAM HEFFERNAN.

The Yellow Boreen.

(DR. PETRIE.)

L.

THE YELLOW BOREEN.*

At the yellow boreen
My heart's secret queen,
Alone on her soft bed is sleeping;
Each tress of her hair,
Than the king's gold more fair,
The dew from the grass might be sweeping.
I watch for her face,
And oh! sad is my case,
For away from her ever I'm sighing:—
And oh! my heart's store,
Be not hard evermore,
Since for love of your beauty I'm dying.

Should my love with me come,
I would build her a home,
The finest e'er told of in Erin;
And 'tis then she would shine,
Like a saint in a shrine,
The palm of all loveliness bearing;
For in your bosom bright
Shines the pure sunny light,
That would bless the poor pilgrim for ever;
And oh!—could I say
You're my own, from this day,
Death's terrors should frighten me never.

Dr. PETRIE.
(Slightly altered.)

* Little Road.

AG AN M-BOITHRÍN BUIDHE.

Ag an m-bóithrín buidhe,
Atá rún mo croidhe,
'N a luidhe air leabainn 'na h-aona
Gach ruibe d'á dlaoi,
Mar ór buidhe an rígh,
Do scaipeas an drúcht do'n fheir ghlas.
Fear do chloinn Taidhg mé,
Bhios dá coímhdeacht,
'Smó a n-galar an bháis dá h-eágmais;
'S a chumainn gheal 's a stor,
Na' biodh ortsa brón
Ag sin buachaill deas óg ad bhreagadh.

Dá bh-faighinn mo rún',
Do dhéanfainn dhé cúirt,
Ba deise da'r dóbhradh a n-Eirinn;
Is do bheith aice an barr
Choidhche 's go bráth,
O fhearaibh is ó mhnáibh ar fhéile.
Mar as ad bhrollach geal ban
'Ta solus gach lá,
Is ní airmhim-si clár geal d'éadain;
Is dá bh feadainn a rádh
Gur tusa mo ghrádh
Nior b'oaglach me ar dháil an eaga.

TRADITIONAL.

SONGS OF THE FOUR NATIONS.

(*Alphabetical Index.*)

Name of Song.	Nationality.	Page.
ALL THROUGH THE NIGHT	WELSH	134
ASH GROVE (THE)	WELSH	180
BLINK OVER THE BURN	SCOTTISH	74
BY THE WATERS OF BABYLON	WELSH	144
BARNEY BRALLAGHAN	IRISH	250
CUPID'S GARDEN	ENGLISH	20
CASTLE OF DROMORE (THE)	IRISH	216
DOUN IN YON BANK	SCOTTISH	62
DIMPLED CHEEK (THE)	WELSH	140
DREAM OF LITTLE RHYS (THE)	WELSH	176
DRIMIN DHU	IRISH	244
FLOODES OF TEARS	ENGLISH	36
GWENLLIAN	WELSH	150
GWILYM AND ELLEN	WELSH	160
GENTLE MAIDEN (THE)	IRISH	200
GAOL OF CLONMEL (THE)	IRISH	238
HAPPY FARMER (THE)	ENGLISH	52
HERE'S TO THY HEALTH	SCOTTISH	66
IN YON GARDEN	SCOTTISH	100
ISLE OF THE HEATHER (THE)	HIGHLAND	110
JENNY'S MANTLE	WELSH	154
KITTY MAGEE	IRISH	204
KATHLEEN NI HOOLIHAUN	IRISH	262
LITTLE MARY CASSIDY	IRISH	232
MY LODGING IT IS ON THE COLD GROUND	ENGLISH	74
MARY JAMIESON	SCOTTISH	82
MISTLETOE (THE)	WELSH	164
MELODY OF MAY (THE)	WELSH	168
MYLE CHARAINE	MANX	188

ALPHABETICAL INDEX.—Continued.

Name of Song.	Nationality.	Page.
Old Towler	English	30
Oh! She's Bonnie	Scottish	70
Opening of the Key (The)	Welsh	122
Pretty Polly Oliver	English	40
Scots Wha Hae	Scottish	78
Slender Boy (The)	Welsh	128
Shule Agra	Irish	210
Snowy-Breasted Pearl (The)	Irish	222
Thou wilt not go and Leave Me Here	English	8
Three Ravens (The)	English	46
The Mackintosh's Lament	Highland	116
Twine the Plaiden	Scottish	88
Tree in the Wood (The)	Irish	254
Ye Mariners of England	English	2
When the King Enjoys His Own Again	English	14
Where be Going?	Cornish	58
Will ye no Come Back Again?	Scottish	94
Were na My Heart Licht	Scottish	104
When in Death	Irish	194
Wild Hills of Clare (The)	Irish	226
Yellow Bokeen (The)	Irish	268

www.ingramcontent.com/pod-product-compliance
Lightning Source LLC
Chambersburg PA
CBHW032101220426
43664CB00008B/1088